Hannah's Gift

Lessons from a Life
Fully Lived

MARIA HOUSDEN

element

Element
An Imprint of HarperCollins*Publishers*
77–85 Fulham Palace Road,
Hammersmith, London W6 8JB

The website address is: www.thorsonselement.co.uk

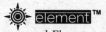

and *Element*
are trademarks of HarperCollins*Publishers* Ltd

First published by Bantam Books 2002
This edition published by Element 2003

1 3 5 7 9 10 8 6 4 2

© Maria Housden 2002

Lines from "On the Beach," by Jane Hirshfield, from
The Lives of the Heart, © 1997. Published by HarperCollins*Publishers*, Inc.
Used by permission of the author.

Lines from "The November Angels," by Jane Hirshfield, from
The October Palace, © 1994. Published by HarperCollins*Publishers*, Inc.
Used by permission of the author.

Lines from *The Essential Rumi,* translated by
Coleman Barks, © 1995. Published by HarperSanFrancisco.
Used by permission of the translator.

Maria Housden asserts the moral right to be
identified as the author of this work

A catalogue record of this book is
available from the British Library

ISBN 0 00 715567 0

Printed and bound in Great Britain by
Clays Ltd, St Ives plc, Bungay

PRAISE FOR *HANNAH'S GIFT*:

'A lyrical, heartbreaking and heartwarming account of a mother's three-year-old daughter's illness and death ... Housden herself offers a real gift to us all with this book.'
Publishers Weekly

'I absolutely could not put *Hannah's Gift* down. It broke my heart and filled me with joy and gave me wisdom for my own daily walk.'
Anne Lamott, author of *Travelling Mercies*

'Maria Housden's testament to a dying daughter's transcendent wisdom, a mother's all-too-earthly devotion, and love's uncanny gift for transforming the greatest suffering into joy and self-awareness, comes as a gift to us all.'
Mark Matousek, author of *Sex Death Enlightenment*

'I love Hannah. I love her hands and her shoes. I love what she knew and knows. I love your book.'
Eve Ensler, activist and playwright, *The Vagina Monologues*

'Superlatives seem pointless; I have only gratitude for the lessons of self-realization emerging here. Read it and weep for the sheer joy of being alive.'
Jeremiah Abrams, author of *Meeting the Shadow*

'*Hannah's Gift* is a celebration of life in all its richness, pain, mystery, and wonder. Maria Housden gives us renewed faith in the transformative power of love.'
John Welwood, author of *Toward a Psychology of Awakening*

'This is a profound and extraordinary book; a small treasure which I'm grateful to have and glad to recommend to anyone who wants to understand how sorrow and joy are inseparable.'
Susan Griffin, author of *A Chorus of Stones*

'Maria Housden gives us the sure knowledge that love not only surrounds us but goes on after death.'
China Galland, author of *The Bond Between Women*

'...Housden's skilful writing and mature understanding of grief make this a spiritually inspiring story about life. Sure you're going to cry. But it's the kind of heart-cracking-open cry that comes from an abundance of feelings: sorrow for this wise and gut-honest narrator; tenderness for Will, the loyal elder brother that Hannah left behind; and love for this baffling, wonderful life that gives us gifts like Hannah.'
Gail Hudson, Spirituality Editor, *Amazon.com*

I dedicate this book to
Will, Hannah, Margaret, and Madelaine
with gratitude and love.

. . . Walk slowly now, small soul, by the edge
of the water. Choose carefully
all you are going to lose,
though any of it would do.

—Jane Hirshfield

Contents

Prologue

The Red Shoes

LOOKING BACK, I REALIZE THAT MY WHOLE LIFE PIVOTS silently around this single moment: I was standing in a Stride-Rite children's shoe store, wondering which pair of shoes to buy. Black or blue leather would coordinate with every outfit in Hannah's preschool wardrobe. I held up one shoe in each color and asked, "Which one do you prefer?"

Hannah had already decided.

"These are *my* shoes," she declared, holding up a pair of red patent leather Mary Janes.

I smiled patiently.

"Hannah, I can only afford to buy one pair of shoes today. Those are lovely, but they're just not practical. We need to buy something that will match the dresses in your closet."

"But Mommy," she protested, "red shoes go with everything. Besides," she added, slipping her feet into the display pair, three sizes too big for her, "they fit me just perfect!!!"

The saleswoman, overhearing the conversation, laughed.

"What do you think, Mom?" the woman asked. "Should I see if we have a smaller size in the back?"

I hesitated. Saving money and making sure my children were properly dressed were things that really mattered to me. Yet something about the expectant joy on Hannah's face lodged the automatic "no" into the back of my throat.

"Yes, why don't you check in the back," I said.

Hannah squealed and jumped up and down. When the woman returned, Hannah slid her feet into the shoes. This time, they *were* a perfect fit. "Just like Cinderella!" Hannah whispered. Walking primly to the mirror, she stood for a moment, transfixed, staring at the image of the shoes on her feet. She turned to me.

"I'd better test them out," she said, tapping the toe of one shoe on the carpeted floor. Not satisfied, she headed for the entrance to the store. The saleswoman and I followed. As soon as Hannah stepped into the atrium of the mall, the sound of the red shoes on the hardwood floor stopped her in her tracks. Pausing, she clicked the heel of one foot and then the other. She looked up, grinning, to see if I had heard. I smiled and nodded encouragingly.

Closing her eyes and extending her arms, Hannah began to dance. Oblivious to everything but the shoes on her feet, she skipped and clicked across the floor, twirling in circles, faster and faster. Her pure delight and the defiant flash of the red shoes caught everyone's attention.

People who passed smiled first at Hannah, then at each other. Some stopped to watch; a few children and an elderly man joined in. One woman, her arms full of shopping bags, turned to the woman next to her. "I've always wanted a pair of red shoes," she said. "Me, too," said the other. "What have we been waiting for?"

Hannah finished her performance by falling in a dramatic heap on the floor. Those who were still watching applauded and cheered. Hannah stood up, smoothed the front of her dress, and adjusted the bow in her hair.

"Mommy," she said, turning to me, "I think these are my shoes, don't you?"

THE TRUEST MEASURE of a life is not its length, but the fullness in which it is lived.

When my daughter Hannah was diagnosed with cancer, one month before her third birthday, everything I had believed about myself and my life was called into question. In the face of the fiercest, most unrelenting truth, I began to look for new answers. Hannah herself became my teacher. Honest, funny, and fearless in the way she lived her life and embraced her death, Hannah opened me to a deeper wisdom, to a more joyful, less fearful way of living.

After Hannah's death in 1994, I began to write about the journey we had taken together. I struggled to remember every detail, afraid to forget even one. It seemed a hopeless, overwhelming task. I gave up, decided to wait, to let myself grieve and heal. Gradually, I began to see that the story was still unfolding; rather than ending with Hannah's death, it had only begun. Now, seven years later, there are certain memories—brief moments that may have taken place weeks or months apart—that stand out in bright relief against the background of my days; moments that continue to live in me because they are still teaching me.

This book is a collection of those memories; a photo album of the moments that became Hannah's gift to me. May her story offer solace to those who suffer, nourishment to those who long for deeper faith, and inspiration to those who want the courage to live their own truth.

Truth

telling it and living it

. . . and the truth shall make you free.

—John 8:32

Dr. Truth Jekyll and
Mr. Hyde Denial

WE BOTH BEGAN BLEEDING ON THE SAME DAY.

I woke to it slowly. Drifting out of a deep sleep, I lay in bed, my eyes closed, inhaling the cool morning air that wafted in through the open window, its breath a welcome respite from the previous night's August heat. I stretched my body and sighed contentedly. Claude stirred beside me. I heard the footfalls of an early morning jogger pass below, on the street side of the house. A car drove by. I opened my eyes. Our bedroom was gray and still.

As I rolled onto my side, I felt a sticky warmth between my legs. Instantly, I was awake. I slid one thigh across the other and felt a sucking sensation as they parted. Clamping my legs together, I closed my eyes and willed myself to be dreaming. Everything was quiet, except for the thud of my heart in my chest. I heard another car drive by; then another. I opened my eyes again, this time more slowly. The first light was beginning to sharpen the outlines of objects in the room.

I ran my hand across my abdomen. Its slightly rounded

fullness reassured me. After all, only yesterday the tiny form of the baby inside had appeared on my doctor's ultrasound screen, filling the room with the pulsing whoosh of its amplified heartbeat. Claude had smiled and squeezed my hand. My whole body had softened with relief. I had miscarried three other pregnancies before this one, all in their eighth week. Yesterday's ultrasound was the confirmation we had been waiting for; this baby, our third child, would be born in March. Will, our son, was five, while Hannah, our daughter, was nearly three.

Last night, I had stood in the nursery, running my hand over the rail of the empty crib, imagining the smell of baby powder in the air again. I slept more deeply than I had in weeks.

Now I lay next to Claude, hyperventilating between wanting to know and not wanting to know. Finally, I slipped out of bed, careful not to brush my thighs against the sheets. When I stood up, I felt a warm trickle run down my leg. I caught the tiny bead on the tip of my finger: blood. I cupped a hand over myself to keep from staining the carpet and tiptoed to the bathroom. Just then, I heard Hannah calling from her bed downstairs.

"Mommy, I have to go potty!"

I grabbed a wad of toilet tissue, wiped my thighs, and glanced at my image in the mirror. My eyes looked wild. I splashed cold water on my face and made my way to Hannah's room. I hardly noticed her sweetness nuzzling the nape of my neck as I carried her to the toilet. I was wondering how I could bear to tell Claude or anyone else about another miscarriage. I felt deeply ashamed; losing this baby meant I had failed again.

When Hannah was finished, I lifted her off the toilet seat and was catapulted out of my grief. Hannah's urine was deep pink: blood. Miscarriages I knew; blood in the urine of a two-year-old I didn't. For an instant, I couldn't think or move. Then a thickness seemed to envelop me; I felt numb but strangely efficient. Everything was happening, but I felt disconnected from any feeling in it. I heard Claude in the bathroom upstairs, running the shower. I dressed Hannah and myself, woke Will, set the table for breakfast and made three phone calls; one to my doctor, one to the pediatrician, and one to my friend Lili. When Claude came downstairs, I told him about the blood, Hannah's and mine. I couldn't even cry. Claude bent over the table, as though he was going to get sick. For thirty seconds, neither of us spoke. Finally he stood up and reached for my hand.

"Honey, what do you want me to do?" he asked. What he was really asking was if I wanted him to miss another day of work. For months, he and the other members of his engineering team had been pushed to the limit, their project overdue and over budget. Three weeks earlier, Claude's boss had demanded that we postpone our family vacation. Claude had refused, explaining that his family was more important than his work. Yesterday he had made the same choice by coming to my appointment with the obstetrician.

"It's okay," I said, taking a deep breath and swallowing

my fear. "I've already arranged for Lili to watch the kids while I go to my appointment, and she's agreed to stay with Will while I take Hannah to hers. We'll be okay. I'll call you as soon as I know anything."

"Are you sure?" Claude asked.

"Definitely," I said, kissing him lightly on the cheek. "Really, it's probably nothing. I'm sure it's going to be fine."

Even as I said it, another part of me watched in silence, knowing what I said wasn't true. It was like being two different characters in the same scene of a movie. In the scene, Hannah and I were bleeding. One part of me felt quiet, accepting of this truth. The other, incapacitated by fear, needed to believe, if only for a while, that everything was going to be okay. I did the only thing I could do: I let both be true.

Silent Comfort

AN HOUR AND A HALF LATER, MY OBSTETRICIAN confirmed what I already knew: The baby inside me was dead. There was nothing but silence in the dark room as she glided the ultrasound wand over my belly; the tiny form that yesterday had a heartbeat and a birthday was nothing but a blot on the blue screen now. Tears pooled in my ears and soaked through the paper sheet beneath me.

"I'm sorry," the doctor said.

I barely nodded to her as I dressed and left the office. In the car, I let the sobs pour out of me. I cried all the way to Lili's house, not only for the life I had lost, but for my fear about what lay ahead.

My friends Kim, Kate, and Deb were at Lili's when I arrived. Our "moms' group" had been meeting every Friday in each other's home for more than a year. The four of them looked up when I came in. My swollen eyes answered their unspoken question. While Lili made lunch, I called Claude and told him about the baby that wouldn't be coming in March; neither of us could think of anything to say. Hanging up the phone, I joined my friends at the table and picked at my food, too numb to talk or eat.

Suddenly, the door to the kitchen opened, and the sounds of children playing spilled into the room. I turned to see Hannah standing on the threshold. She was wearing a sundress, a pink headband, and her new red shoes. She stood there quietly looking at me. Then she crossed the room, crawled into my lap, and began gently stroking my cheeks.

Perspective

TWO HOURS LATER, HANNAH DUMPED A BASKETFUL OF hand puppets onto the floor of the pediatrician's office and sorted through the pile until she found the one she was looking for. Tucking a butterfly under her arm, she climbed into my lap, while I gazed absently at the diplomas and photographs on the wall. Already I felt relieved. Minutes before, Dr. Edman had gently examined her. His face hadn't registered any concern. He had asked us to wait for him in his office, standard procedure, while he made a phone call. Now he came through the door and sat on the edge of his desk.

"Is it possible for you to reach Claude at work?" he asked.

My brain struggled to register what he had just said. This was *not* standard procedure. What could be so important that I needed to call Claude?

"Hannah has a mass in her abdomen," Dr. Edman said gently. "I've called the emergency room. They're expecting you; Claude should meet you there."

I dialed the phone and, when Claude answered, repeated Dr. Edman's words.

"What does this mean?" Claude asked.

"I have no idea," I said.

Hannah slept in her car seat in the back while I drove. Forty minutes later, as I pulled into the emergency room parking lot and shut off the engine, I realized that I couldn't remember stopping for one light or stop sign all the way there. Either I had driven through every one, or I was simply too dazed to remember. As I unbuckled Hannah and lifted her out, a question pierced through the fog in my brain: Could a mass be cancer? I dismissed it immediately. How could I possibly *think* such a thing? Two-year-olds don't get cancer. Dr. Edman had said it was a mass. We would get it out, as simple as that.

As the automatic doors to the emergency room swung open, I felt better almost immediately. A nurse bustled toward me.

"Mrs. Martell?" she asked, partly a question, partly a greeting.

I nodded. Hannah lifted her head drowsily from my shoulder.

"It's okay, Missy," I whispered. "We're at the hospital. These people are going to help us figure out what's happening with your tummy."

"I'm hungry," Hannah said, closing her eyes and laying her head back on my shoulder.

The nurse led us to a small examining room. I sat Hannah next to me on the edge of the padded table. The nurse took Hannah's blood pressure and temperature and then asked me to remove Hannah's dress.

"No, Mommy, it's too cold," Hannah said.

I turned to the nurse, who shrugged her shoulders.

"I guess she can leave it on," she said.

Within minutes, a parade of doctors, nurses, residents, and technicians filed in, asked questions, took notes, and left, closing the door behind them. My sense of relief at being there was fading. I wanted Claude. I opened the door to the hall and startled a group of residents and nurses who were speaking in loud, conspiratorial whispers outside our room. I looked past them and saw Claude coming toward me, almost running, his head whipping from one side to the other as he read the numbers above the doors to each room. He looked panicked and disoriented, no more capable of knowing what to do than I was.

"Daddy," Hannah exclaimed as Claude came into the room. He and I embraced quickly.

An efficient-looking resident poked his head into the room.

"In ten minutes, Hannah is scheduled for X-rays downstairs. An aide will be by to pick her up."

"Mommy, I want you to come with me," Hannah said.

"Of course, Missy," I replied.

The resident looked at me sternly. "You can go downstairs with her," he said, "but you can't go in the room unless you're sure you're not pregnant."

My voice sounded far away when I answered. "I'm definitely not pregnant," I heard myself say.

What had felt like the deepest loss hours ago was now enabling me to do the one thing I wanted more than anything else: to be with Hannah. Only my perspective had changed; the truth, that the baby inside me was dead, was the same, either way.

Light in the Shadow

❧

THE DOCTOR CAME INTO THE ROOM, FLIPPED THE SWITCH on the light board, and slid the film under the clip. I shifted Hannah's sleeping body to my other hip and leaned in next to Claude to get a closer look. The doctor used his pen to point to a large, dark shadow beneath the white outline of Hannah's ribs.

"There it is."

The pieces were beginning to fall into place. Three weeks earlier, during our vacation in Michigan, we had taken Hannah to an emergency room. She had been complaining that it hurt to lie down; she moaned in her sleep and ran a slight fever at night. The doctor told us she had the flu and sent us away with a sample-size packet of Children's Tylenol. Two days later, when she didn't seem to be getting any better, we took her to another hospital. The pediatrician there ordered X-rays of Hannah's chest to rule out pneumonia, and then tried to examine Hannah's abdomen. Hannah screamed and refused to lie down, saying it hurt too much. The doctor gave up, obviously exasperated.

"There's nothing wrong with her; she's just manipulating you," the woman told us. "She's a typical two-year-old who doesn't want to go to sleep."

"How can we be sure it's not something more serious?" I asked, somewhat distracted. Will and Hannah, bored with waiting, had stepped outside the examining room and were now shrieking and chasing each other in the hall.

The doctor sniffed disapprovingly at the commotion.

"Well, look at her," the doctor said. "She has too much energy to be really sick. A sick child would be listless and lethargic, would run a fever all day, not just at night. She wouldn't put up such a fuss during an examination. If you want, make an appointment with her pediatrician when you get home; but as far as I can see, she's fine."

I felt confused and embarrassed by the doctor's words. Every bone in my body was telling me something was wrong, and yet, perhaps the doctor was right; maybe I *was* just the inadequate mother of an overindulged child. While Claude rounded up Will and Hannah, I quickly collected our things. Escorting our two unruly children past the other, obviously sick children in the waiting room, I felt guilty for having wasted a doctor's valuable time.

Now, looking at the dark shadow on the X-ray of Hannah's ribs, I felt like a profound failure again. The doctor in Michigan had only been half right; instead of being the inadequate mother of an overindulged child, I was the inadequate mother of a very sick one. Why hadn't I trusted myself more? The doctors knew symptoms of illness as they applied generally to children. I knew Hannah. We were authorities on different subjects. I should have insisted that the doctor's explanation of Hannah's behavior didn't match what I knew to be true for her. Hannah had no interest in playing games to get what she wanted; she asked for it directly, demanding it if necessary. And why was she moaning in her sleep and running fevers at night? Even if these were unusual symptoms, surely they were signs of something more than manipulative behavior! Was I so afraid of making a mistake, so afraid of what these strangers might think of me, that I had failed my daughter?

As the doctor peeled the film from the light board, I knew one thing: I was going to have to start speaking up, before it was too late for Hannah. Before it was too late for me.

Just One Thing

❦

IT WAS PAST MIDNIGHT, BUT NOT DARK OR QUIET. THE hallway's fluorescent light spilled into the room through the half-open door. A monitor beeped; the IV pump clicked. If I lay still enough, I could almost hear the whoosh of the pain medication pulsing through the line that fed a tiny vein in Hannah's hand. Because of it, Hannah was sleeping peacefully for the first time in weeks.

Although my eyes were burning with fatigue, they wouldn't stay shut. I began to wonder if I was caught in one of those dreams where you think you're awake but you're not. Hannah, curled up on her side next to me, stirred. I sat up, peering at her face in the half-light. Her skin was so pale. I ran my finger along her cheek and brushed a few strands of blond hair away from her lips. Rearranging the blankets, I smiled to see that her new red shoes were still on her feet. Ever since we'd bought them two days before, she had refused to take them off. As I lay back down, Hannah lifted her arm and dropped it lazily across my chest.

I couldn't remember if I had ever lived a day as never-ending as this one. After more than seven hours of tests, questions, and examinations, the emergency room doctors had finally moved Hannah into a room on the pediatric floor. At first the nurses had said I couldn't stay overnight; there was nowhere for me to sleep. When Claude and I insisted, they agreed to make an exception and let Hannah and me sleep together in her twin-size bed.

Before Claude left, I handed him a list of things that Hannah and I would need in the coming days: Hannah's pink-flowered nightgown that she called her "robe j's," a pair of leggings and a sweatshirt for me, underwear, tooth-brushes, toothpaste, and Hannah's pink blanket. In the midst of a crisis, our needs were surprisingly simple.

Later, I sat on the edge of the bed and dialed a series of phone numbers I knew by heart. First I called our parents, Claude's and my own. I told them briefly about Hannah and the miscarriage and asked them to call the rest of the family. My mother agreed to come as soon as possible to help with Will. Then I called everyone I could think of who was expecting me to do something for them in the coming year: church committees, the PTA, Will's school. I told them that Hannah was sick, that I would be devoting all my time and energy to being with her and our family, that I was no longer available for anything else. I felt as if I had lost a thousand pounds.

I realized that for years I had been measuring my worth by being involved, important, and indispensable, saying "yes" to things not only because I wanted to be helpful, but because I wanted to be looked up to, admired, and loved. I had poured myself into maintaining an illusion of perfection in every aspect of my life. And I had been so busy "doing the right thing" for the benefit of everyone else that I had lost track of what really mattered to me.

Now, lying in the half-dark, my priorities seemed incredibly clear; this was where I wanted and needed to be. I felt so certain about it that, for the first time in a long time, I forgot to worry about what anyone else thought.

Respect

I STRUGGLED TO ROUSE MYSELF FROM A DENSE, DREAMLESS sleep. My alarm clock was beeping. Reaching for the snooze button, my arm brushed against a cold metal rail. My eyes flew open. The beep wasn't coming from an alarm clock; it was coming from the pump of an IV.

I sat up slowly, feeling as if I had passed through an invisible fold in the universe and landed in some altered state of reality. Hannah was still asleep. I glanced around, wondering what time it was. The light coming through the slatted blinds looked early-morning gray, but the clatter and conversation in the hall suggested it might be later than I thought.

A nurse strode purposefully into the room, followed by a heavyset young woman in blue carrying a tray of flying saucers. While the nurse busied herself with the beeping IV, the young woman set the tray down and lifted the flying saucers to reveal our breakfast: colorless oatmeal, lukewarm scrambled eggs, and cold toast.

"The first day of meals is the worst," she explained

apologetically. "Since you weren't here yesterday to choose, we have to give you what's left. Tomorrow's menu is under the plate. Circle what you want. I'll be back in a while to pick it up."

She glanced at Hannah's sleeping form. "We can only bring one tray per patient, so you might want to circle extra items. We'll do our best to bring what we can."

She turned to leave, squeezing through a crowd of white-coated residents that had congregated in the hallway outside our door. Three of them came in. Each wore a stethoscope and carried a clipboard. As they approached Hannah's bed, two of them cleared their throats at the same time and then laughed self-consciously. The nurse, who was finished with the IV pole, nodded to them as she left.

I eyed the residents suspiciously. One of the things I was beginning to understand about the hospital was that we rarely saw the same person twice. It was disconcerting, too, that while they knew so much about us, we knew almost nothing about them. Hannah opened her eyes and sat up.

"Mommy, who are all these people?" she asked, frowning.

One of the residents spoke. "We need to examine her," he said efficiently. "It'll only take a minute."

"My name is Hannah," Hannah said quietly.

"Yes, of course," he answered. He stepped closer, reaching for his stethoscope. As he did, the two residents next to him moved in, and then those in the hall entered and formed a semicircle around the bed.

"Stop!" Hannah yelled, holding out her arm like a policeman in traffic. The resident with the stethoscope froze. Hannah turned to me.

"Mommy, please ask these people to leave. They aren't my friends; they didn't even tell me their names!"

I paused. The residents were looking at me. I knew they were counting on me to tell Hannah to be a good little girl and let them do what they needed to do. I remembered the Michigan doctor's diagnosis: manipulative, overindulged two-year-old. I realized these doctors might think the same thing. I didn't care; if any person in this world deserved respect, it was Hannah. I looked at the guy with the stethoscope.

"She's right," I told him.

The resident frowned and tapped a finger absently on his clipboard. The other residents shifted their gaze to him.

"I have to examine you, Hannah," he said finally. "Will you let me do it if I tell you my name?"

Hannah narrowed her eyes and looked first at him and then at me.

"Okay," she said finally, "but all those other people have to leave."

He nodded. The others turned and filed out of the room. When the last person had left, the resident raised his stethoscope and leaned over Hannah. She stopped him.

"What's your name?" she asked.

"Dr. Fiorelli," he said, smiling.

"No, your *real* name," she said, totally exasperated.

"Tony," he replied, grinning now from ear to ear.

"Oh, Dr. Tony," she said, settling back on the pillows. "That's a *nice* name."

Dr. Tony must have spread the word. From that day on, no more than three or four residents entered Hannah's room at a time, and everyone who did introduced themselves to her using their *real* names.

Dr. Markoff's Rule

DR. MARKOFF CLEARED HIS THROAT AND ADJUSTED HIS glasses. He was Dr. Edman's partner, one of Hannah's pediatricians. He was sitting on the edge of his chair across from Claude and me. His shoulders were stooped, his face gaunt and strained. His wiry hair was disheveled, two-day-old creases wrinkled his trousers, and his shirt was missing one of its buttons. He didn't seem to notice or care.

"I'm speaking to you as a father, not as a pediatrician," he began, leaning forward so his elbows rested on his knees. He cleared his throat again; I studied him more carefully. He looked as if he was about to cry.

Claude and I exchanged glances.

"My daughter Danielle was diagnosed with leukemia last year. She's two years old. My wife is with her now at the Mayo Clinic in Minnesota, where she's getting a stem cell transplant. We're trying to save her life."

In one breath we went from a gathering of two parents and a doctor to two fathers and a mother who belonged to a club no one wanted to be in.

"You are going to have to make thousands of decisions from now on that no one but the two of you can make; some of them may make a difference whether Hannah lives or dies. The best advice I can give you is this."

He looked directly at Claude and me.

"Make the best decision you can with the information you have *at that time*." He leaned back and ran his fingers through his hair.

" 'At that time' is the critical part. You'll see what I mean. You can drive yourself crazy saying, 'If only we had known this, if only we had known that.' The point is, you *didn't* know, so just keep telling yourselves, 'We did the best we could with what we knew. We did the best we could with what we knew.' "

I could hear a deep truth in his words. As I let them seep into my heart, something softened in me and fell away. I realized that Dr. Markoff's rule applied not only to the decisions we had to make about Hannah's treatment, but to every other area of my life as well. My fear of making mistakes could no longer paralyze me; from now on, it would be enough to do the best I could with what I knew.

Truth:
A Special Medicine

WILL WAS CURLED UP ON MY LAP, OUR ARMCHAIR touching the side of Hannah's bed. His blond crew cut tickled the bottom of my chin. His body had been long and solid from the day he was born, but it was his soft green eyes that most people noticed first and remembered.

Hannah was watching us from the bed, propped against a pile of pillows. A plastic line ran from her arm to an IV pole. She had spread her pink blanket over her legs and was wearing a rhinestone crown and her pink-flowered "robe j's."

I cleared my throat. The weight of the moment crushed against my chest.

"Hannah, the doctors have figured out why you are feeling so sick. There is a lump in your tummy called a tumor. A tumor happens sometimes when a few of the cells in a person's body grow the wrong way and don't do what they're supposed to do. The doctors are going to take it out, and then give you medicines to try to make sure the bad cells don't come back."

"Is it going to hurt?" Hannah asked, her brow wrinkled and her lips pursed into a worried pout. I paused. In the past, I had often coped with difficult situations by glossing over them, trying to find something good in them, praying that if I could avoid the truth long enough, it would go away. This time, though, I wanted Will and Hannah to be able to trust me. I couldn't start lying to them now.

"Yes, Hannah, it probably will hurt, but the doctors and nurses are going to do everything they can to make it hurt as little as possible. They have special medicines that will make you sleep while they take the lump out, and other medicines that will help your body rest while it gets better."

"I don't want to sleep. I'm not tired!!" Hannah protested.

"You don't have to sleep now," Will said gently, "only when they take the lump out. Right, Mom?" he asked, turning to me.

I smiled and nodded.

"Oh. *That's* okay." Hannah sighed, sounding relieved.

"Mom." Will was still looking at me, his eyes filling with tears. "Is a tumor the same thing as cancer?"

"We don't know yet, Will," I said, starting to cry. "The doctors can't be sure until they take it out and look at the cells under a microscope."

Hannah was watching us silently.

"If it's bad news you'll tell us, right, Mom?" Will asked.

Hannah sat straight up and looked into my eyes without blinking. I took a breath. I couldn't help wishing that Claude had been able to be here with me, but he had told

me he didn't trust himself to know what to say. I appreciated his honesty, and I also knew that if ever there was a
time when the two of us had to respect our differences, this
was it. We were like two people in a one-man life raft in
the middle of a dark ocean.

Will and Hannah were still waiting for my answer.

"Yes, Will," I said. "Even if it's bad news, I'll tell you the
truth."

Hannah smiled and leaned back into her pillows.

"Thanks, Mom," Will said, flinging his arms around my
neck.

"Mommy, I love you," Hannah said.

"I love you both," was all I could say.

Love in the Dark

OUR WORLD HAD SHRUNK TO THE SIZE OF A HOSPITAL floor, but I didn't mind. My brain was busy replacing no longer needed facts, such as the cost of a package of diapers, with new ones, such as the proper doses of certain medications; it didn't have room for much else.

Hannah was restless. We decided to go for a stroll through our new neighborhood. As she swung her legs over the side of the bed, I lunged to untangle the IV tube from the toe of her shoe before her foot hit the floor.

"Wait a minute, Missy," I said, leaning over to unplug the IV pump. The unit began to beep. I pushed the "silence" button and wound the power cord around the pole.

"Hurry up, Mommy," Hannah exclaimed, hopping from one foot to the other. "I hear Baby Shondra crying. I think she wants her mommy."

I wheeled the IV pole away from the wall and checked to make sure the tube wasn't caught on anything.

"Okay, we're ready," I said.

Hannah held my hand in one of hers, and with the other

lifted the edge of her nightgown like a princess, to keep the hem from dragging on the floor. We walked slowly as I maneuvered the awkward equipment into the hallway and followed our usual route. Turning right out of her room, we strolled past the supply closet and the conference room, stopping in front of the open doors of the pediatric intensive care unit. It was empty now, but not for long.

"Remember, Hannah, here's where you're going to wake up after your surgery tomorrow."

Hannah took a couple of steps into the room. I followed. Respirators, monitors, breathing tubes, and carts of medical supplies lined the walls. The room smelled like an emergency. It was hard for me to imagine Hannah there. I forced myself to do it.

"You'll be in one of these beds, and I'll be sleeping next to you in the big blue chair. Some tubes will be connected to your body to help you breathe, and some to help you sleep. There will be lots of beeping and other noises. A nurse will be with us all the time to make sure everything is okay."

"I want Nurse Katie or Nurse Amy," Hannah said, "and I want to wear my red shoes to surgery. Be sure to tell the doctors that."

"I'll tell them, Hannah, but I'm not sure they can do it."

"Well, that's not fair," she cried, stomping her foot on the linoleum floor. "Surgery has too many rules. I can't eat dinner. I can't wear my robe j's. I can't wear my red shoes. That's not fair," she repeated.

"I see what you mean, Hannah. That is a lot of rules. I'll tell them what you said and see what they can do."

We continued our walk; past the playroom, around the corner, stopping briefly to choose a book from the library shelves, and then around the corner again. This was the busiest street in the neighborhood: room after room of sick children and their families. A few parents looked up as we passed, exchanging wan, dazed, or sympathetic glances with me. Each room was a story in itself. I never tried to figure out who was here for what. My own story was enough. Hannah's pace quickened. I struggled to keep up, the IV pole clattering along beside me. The nurses exclaimed in unison when they saw Hannah coming.

"Baby Shondra has been missing you," Nurse Patty called from behind the desk.

A tiny baby was lying in a bassinet in front of the nurses' station, her cries lost in the flurry of activity. She was two months old, with translucent blue eyes, dark brown curls, and pursed rosebud lips. She had also been declared severely brain-damaged; she would never be able to see or hear.

Her parents had explained to the nurses that they could not care for such a baby.

The hospital had filed the necessary paperwork, but until a foster home was found, she slept in the hospital hall. Busy nurses fed, changed, rocked, and held her whenever they could. Mostly, when she wasn't sleeping, Shondra cried.

"It's okay, Baby Shondra," Hannah murmured, leaning over the edge of the bassinet, close to the baby's screwed-up, bawling face. "Your mommy will be back soon. And guess what," she added brightly, "I brought you something to read."

Shondra's cries became whimpers. Hannah stroked Shondra's cheeks and poked her finger through Shondra's clenched fist. Shondra stopped crying. The nurses looked away as I lifted Shondra out of her bassinet. I knew that they weren't supposed to allow me to pick her up, but they were grateful for the help. As I cuddled the baby close to my chest, I couldn't help wondering if her parents felt as disappointed by life as I did. Weren't bad things only supposed to happen to bad people? What had I done, what had these little girls done, to deserve this?

Hannah was already sitting on the floor, her back against the wall, waiting. I sat down carefully next to her and laid Baby Shondra across our laps. Hannah picked up her library book and opened it to the first page.

"Once upon a time there was a princess," she began, making up her favorite story as she pretended to read.

Then, turning the book around, she held the page open, inches from Shondra's face.

"See, Baby Shondra, see? It's a beautiful princess, just like you and me."

She turned to me and grinned. I kissed the top of her head.

"I love you, Missy," I whispered.

"I know, Mommy. I know," she whispered back.

As I sat on the floor, listening to Hannah spin tales into Shondra's soundless world, I realized that I, too, had been telling stories to deaf ears. The truth didn't care about my expectations, about the way things were supposed to be. It was what it was. As in the moment in the emergency room, when my miscarriage had become the reason I could go with Hannah to her X-rays, I was reminded that it is my expectations, the story I weave around the truth, that make what is happening seem better or worse, good or bad, fair or not fair.

Looking at Baby Shondra, now asleep on Hannah's lap, I realized something else, too. Hannah's sense that every little girl was precious and loved wasn't just a fantasy she had made up; it had emerged out of a deeper truth. Love *is* bigger than tumors or blindness, and it was a feeling that Hannah trusted and knew.

Room for the Truth

🖋

THERE WAS A FLURRY OF ACTIVITY IN THE PREOPERATING room. Efficient-looking people in official-looking coats were bustling back and forth around us. The huge metal doors of the operating room swung open and shut, and the anesthesiologist appeared.

Hannah's body was limp in my lap. Her eyes were open, but they rolled lazily around in their sockets. She was wrapped in her pink blanket, wearing nothing but her red shoes. An hour earlier she had refused to wear a hospital gown.

"It's not pretty, and it doesn't match my shoes," she had said.

"How's she doing?" the anesthesiologist asked, wrapping her fingers around Hannah's wrist, feeling her pulse.

"My shoes," Hannah said weakly.

"What did she say?" the doctor asked.

"Hannah's worried you're going to take off her shoes," Claude explained. "She made a deal with the surgeon that she could wear them in surgery."

"Oh, I heard about that," the anesthesiologist said. "You must be a very special patient, Hannah. Dr. Saad gave us specific orders that you be allowed to wear your red shoes. I won't forget."

Hannah nodded and closed her eyes. The doctor pushed another syringe of sedative into the IV line. Hannah's head dropped against my chest with a thud. I held my breath as long as I could. Hannah didn't move. The operating room doors swung open again, and two nurses wheeled a long gurney covered with a white sheet into the room. One of them leaned over, gathered Hannah's body in her arms, and lifted her off my lap. Laying Hannah in the middle of the white sheet, the nurse covered the lower half of her body with a hospital blanket.

My eyes studied Hannah, looking for any sign that she was aware of being taken from me. She didn't flinch. She looked tiny, lost in the middle of the huge white expanse. I struggled to keep from believing she might already be dead. This was the first time in five days she'd been more than an arm's length away from me. A sob broke out of my chest. Claude held me as we watched the nurses push Hannah's gurney toward the operating room. The doors parted to let Hannah and her attendants through, then swung shut behind them. Claude and I didn't move, barely able to believe what was happening. A minute later, the doors swung open and one of the nurses appeared. She handed me Hannah's shoes, wrapped in a clear plastic bag.

"She was completely sedated before we took them off,"

she said. "Make sure the recovery nurse gets them, so we can put them on before she wakes up."

She smiled sympathetically.

"She's in good hands. It'll be okay," she said softly before walking away.

Claude and I were led to a curtained alcove in the family waiting area. There was no room in that tiny space for anything but two chairs and the truth.

The first hour we sobbed uncontrollably in each other's arms. When there were no tears left, we began to talk. For years, I had loved Claude as deeply and imperfectly as I was able. From the moment we met, I had been drawn to him like a little boy's finger to the tip of a flame. He had seemed wise and mature compared with the other men/boys I knew. He was earnest, hardworking, and handsome. He also seemed deeply hurt and unusually angry sometimes. I was, too. There had been something about our mutual hopes and hurts that had brought us together. We had married while I was still in college, when he was twenty-five and I was twenty.

As we clung to each other and waited for news from the surgeon, Claude and I knew one thing: Our children were more important than anything else either of us would ever do. They were the reason we were together, and we wanted to have more. It was a truth so deep that it cut cleanly through any doubts or fears we might otherwise have had.

"Let's get pregnant again as soon as we can," Claude said. With my face buried in his shoulder, I nodded.

A Mustard Seed

LAURAJANE, THE NEW PASTOR OF OUR SMALL METHODIST church, was standing across from me on the other side of Hannah's bed. She didn't look like any church leader I had ever seen. She was thirty-one, the same age as me, with a short, thick body and a head of wiry red curls that refused to be tamed. She wore a long, green velvet dress, and a gold cross hung from a chain around her neck. She clutched a wad of tissue in her hand, because her eyes kept filling with tears.

Two days before, surgeons had lifted a tumor the size of a small soccer ball from Hannah's abdomen. Now she was lying on the bed, tethered to a respirator and heavily sedated. Plastic tubes and the tips of her red shoes emerged from the edges of her pink blanket. Monitors with zigzagging green lines hung from the ceiling above the bed. The only sounds in the room were an occasional beep and a periodic whoosh from the respirator.

Laurajane bowed her head and started to pray. I closed my eyes and tried to quiet my mind. It was doing crazy things. In one moment it was a model of efficiency, deciphering the whooshes, clicks, and beeps of the various machines so quickly that they no longer frightened me. In the next, I couldn't even remember when I had last eaten.

I desperately needed someone to take care of me. Since Hannah's surgery, I hadn't slept more than a few hours at a time, and yesterday my body had given up the tiny form of our dead baby. I knew that I couldn't depend on Claude to do any more. After five days of juggling work, errands, phone calls, visiting me and Hannah, and shuttling Will between the hospital, play dates, and home, he was as exhausted as I was.

At least my mother was now here. She and Will were moving into the Ronald McDonald House, a beautiful facility with lots of toys and activities to keep Will busy, across the street from the hospital. Claude would continue to sleep at home. It was probably just as well; he and my mother had, over the years, only barely managed to get along, and these days I couldn't handle being a referee.

One of the monitors began to beep. I realized my mind had been wandering. The beeping stopped. I tried once again to concentrate on Laurajane's words. It was too late.

"Amen," Laurajane said.

I opened my eyes. Tears were streaming down Laurajane's cheeks and dripping off her chin. She was looking at me as if she was about to say something; I didn't yet know her well enough to imagine what it might be. For days, people had been telling me, "God only gives us what we can handle." I hoped Laurajane wasn't about to tell me the same thing. I knew these words were meant to comfort me, but I was finding it difficult to accept that what was happening to Hannah and our family was part of some benevolent God's plan. I also suspected that when people said this, they were secretly comforting themselves, imagining that since *they* couldn't handle what was happening to us, their God would never give it to them.

"I have no choice!" I wanted to scream. I couldn't wall myself off from pain and fear. To turn away from them would be to turn away from Hannah. No matter how bad things were, I wasn't willing to do that.

Laurajane cleared her throat and reached for another tissue.

"I'm sorry," she said softly, pausing to blow her nose, "but I can't lie to you. I want more than anything to make sense of what is happening to you guys, but I can't even begin to pretend that this is something I understand.

"I became a minister because I loved and believed in God and wanted to help other people, but now, seeing what you are going through, I'm not sure I have what it takes. This whole scene doesn't jibe with what I thought I knew about Him; it's hard to believe that the God I love would let a child suffer like this."

I couldn't decide whether to kiss her or fall on my knees. Laurajane's humility and willingness to acknowledge out loud the unfairness and insanity I was feeling came as a profound relief. I realized then that what I needed most wasn't for someone to make me feel better; I needed people like Laurajane who were willing to stand with me in the face of the raw truth.

A Deeper Silence

CLAUDE AND I WERE SITTING ON FADED PLASTIC CHAIRS IN an old supply closet that was posing as a conference room. Dr. Kamalaker and his partner, Dr. Bekele, shuffled through folders and papers that were strewn on the table in front of them. They were pediatric oncologists who worked for the children's clinic attached to the hospital and were now officially in charge of Hannah's case. A nurse sat to one side with Jill, the clinic's social worker, trying desperately but unsuccessfully to appear relaxed. Claude and I held hands and sat so close together that the legs of our chairs overlapped.

Dr. Kamalaker lifted a long printed sheet from the pile in front of him.

"We got the report from the lab in California," he said softly, raising his head to look first at Claude and then at me.

I felt very, very quiet; I knew the truth was coming in a way I had never known it before.

Claude squeezed my hand tighter and leaned in to me until he was almost sitting on the edge of my chair. The nurse looked away. Jill crossed her legs.

Something was happening. I could feel the weight of my body pressing my tailbone into the seat of the chair. I felt breath pouring in and out of my lungs, and my heart pounding in my chest, but my awareness had expanded beyond my body and thoughts. Although my eyes never left Dr. Kamalaker's, I had a sense of being able to see the whole room, then Hannah in her room down the hall, and then the whole hospital block. Eventually I saw everyone I loved and everything else, until the whole universe was contained in one place.

"The news is not as good as we had hoped. The tumor *is* cancerous; it's called a Rhabdoid tumor of the kidney. It's malignant, aggressive, and rare, but there's still about a twenty-percent chance of remission. We've been in touch with a hospital in Washington State that has been treating a little girl who was diagnosed fifteen months ago. That's good news, since most patients die within a year."

He paused. The room was still. Someone's chair scraped across the floor. A throat cleared. Four pairs of eyes watched us. As the silence grew, the nurse turned her gaze politely, painfully away. Claude stared straight ahead and said nothing.

As quiet as the room was, there was a deeper silence in me; my heart had jumped beyond the diagnosis, beyond the prognosis, beyond the treatment. *I knew that Hannah was going to die, and I was not afraid.*

I do not know where my fear went. I simply knew that if Hannah was going to die, I needed to face the truth and make the most of the time we had left. I also knew that when it was time, I wanted her home, to let her go as gently as she could go.

I opened my mouth and let the question fall out of my heart.

"Dr. Kamalaker, when it's clear that Hannah has had enough, when she's ready to die, will you help her go?"

Claude turned to look at me. Everyone else did, too. Dr. Kamalaker studied me thoughtfully without answering.

Dr. Bekele spoke. "You realize, don't you, that we are not giving up hope that Hannah's cancer can go into remission. We intend to do everything we can to help her." Jill and the nurse nodded emphatically in agreement.

I knew they were probably horrified by my question; part of me was stunned by it, too. Even if I knew in my heart that Hannah was going to die, wouldn't saying it out loud clinch the deal? I didn't think so. I wasn't giving up on the possibility that Hannah could be cured. I was simply acknowledging something that is already true for everyone: Death comes to all of us, ready or not. To know that Hannah was going to die couldn't *cause* her death any more than denying it could *prevent* her death. The truth was going to be what it was, either way. The only choice I had was to decide what I was going to do with it.

Dr. Kamalaker and I were still looking at each other. His eyes were soft and sympathetic. I felt as if he was seeing into my heart.

"I am not willing to give up in the face of this disease," he said finally. "I am going to do everything I can to beat this cancer, but if we are not successful, I am also willing to help you with what you asked."

Waves of relief surged through me; not only had I been able to give a voice to my deepest fear, but I had found someone else willing to face the truth with me. If Hannah was going to die, I now knew that I wasn't going to be alone in it.

Resilience

DOCTORS HAD GRADUALLY DECREASED THE AMOUNT OF Hannah's sedative and then removed the respirator tube from her throat. After all she had just been through, I couldn't believe how good she looked. Although she had lost a lot of weight, her voice was hoarse, and the skin on her cheeks was raw where strips of tape had held the breathing tube in place, Hannah had spent the day laughing, talking, sipping juice, and watching videos with Will. I had even managed to wash her hair, using a plastic bowl and a sample of baby shampoo that one of the nurses had scrounged around to find for me. Hannah had insisted that we pull it back into a huge pink bow.

Now, she was about to eat her first solid food in over a week.

"Dinner!" the nurse announced with a flourish, lifting the lids on the tray in front of her to reveal a plate of mashed potatoes, cups of Jell-O and pudding, and a bowl of chicken broth.

Hannah frowned. She wasn't impressed. She poked her

finger into the potatoes, and then folded her arms across her chest.

"No way, José. I'm not eating *that*. I want pizza," she said. The nurse smiled.

"Hannah, the doctors ordered these foods for you because they will be gentle on your throat and tummy. Tomorrow, maybe, you can have pizza."

Hannah looked steadily at her for about ten seconds. The nurse didn't move.

"Get Dr. Tony," Hannah said.

When Dr. Tony arrived, the nurse explained the situation. Dr. Tony tapped a finger on his clipboard the way he had that first morning when Hannah had stopped him in his tracks. He looked at Hannah. She returned his gaze.

"Well," he said finally, "I *am* Italian, so I know why Hannah feels the way she does about pizza. If I hadn't eaten anything in a really long time, I'd want pizza, too."

Twenty minutes later, a second tray was delivered from the cafeteria. The nurse set it on the table in front of Hannah. Dr. Tony peeked his head into the room and winked at me, grinning from ear to ear.

"Ta-da!" Hannah said, lifting the lid. She let out a shriek, and I saw the reason for Dr. Tony's grin.

There, in the middle of the tray, sat two slices of pizza *and* a dish of chocolate ice cream.

The Scent of Home

EXACTLY TWO WEEKS AFTER I HAD CARRIED HANNAH across the parking lot to the emergency room, we brought her home. It was a lovely late-summer evening when we pulled into the driveway. While Will and Hannah clapped and cheered, some part of me wanted to turn and run. Hannah's cancer and my life had somehow felt more manageable in the hospital. Now, looking at the relief on Claude's face as he unloaded the suitcases from the car, I imagined he was expecting things to return to normal. The problem was, I couldn't remember what "normal" looked like anymore.

Stepping through the front door of our house, even the smell was different than I remembered. As I wandered from one room to the next, I saw my life through new eyes. I wondered what had happened to the woman who used to live here; it was hard to believe it had ever been me. I realized that my old routine—Friday morning moms' group, play dates for the kids, church on Sunday—was a beautiful life for someone else, but not for me. I had no idea what my life was; I simply knew it wasn't this.

Hannah seemed tentative, too. She walked slowly into the house, climbed the stairs, and stood quietly in the doorway of her room. Will came bounding up behind her, his arms full of the dolls, books, and stuffed animals people had sent to the hospital.

"Hannah, let's find a place to put your new things," he said.

"Okay," she agreed.

While Claude finished unloading the car, I began clearing a shelf in the laundry room to make way for boxes of gauze, tape, antiseptics, vials of saline and heparin, syringes, caps, and a bright red container that read "Hazardous Materials—Medical Waste." Where I once had a hospital floor of doctors, nurses, and residents to care for Hannah, I now had a space above the washer and dryer.

I heard peals of laughter coming from Hannah's room.

Peeking in, I saw the contents of Hannah's dress-up box strewn all over the floor. In the process of unpacking Hannah's things, Will had found a short, blond wig. He was wearing it now, with Hannah's rhinestone crown, dancing around the room, his solid boy body packed into a tutu with electric-blue sequins and a shimmering, multi-colored skirt. Hannah was doubled over on the floor, laughing so hard she couldn't stand up. I started to laugh, too. Claude, hearing the commotion, bounded up the stairs and joined in.

Listening to our laughter, I was filled with relief that we were together, that we could experience this much love and joy in such an ordinary moment. I realized, then, that home is not some familiar place you can always return to; it is the rightness you feel, *wherever* you are, when you know that you are loved.

Beyond Fear

THE TWO OF US WERE CROSSING THE PARKING LOT, ON OUR way to Hannah's second chemotherapy appointment. It was early September, about a week before her third birthday. Her red shoes tapped on the pavement as she walked beside me. She was carrying her Little Mermaid lunch box, packed with graham crackers and apple juice. I held her other hand, mindful of the cars that were looking for spaces in the busy lot.

"Mommy, do children ever die?"

She asked the question with the same tone she might have used if she had wanted to know where babies come from, without a trace of fear or concern. Her face was turned toward me, waiting for my response. I forgot about the cars in the parking lot and the IV equipment waiting for us upstairs. Hannah's question sucked me, fully present, into my body.

I paused before answering. I wished I could tell her that children didn't die, or that, even if they did, it was so unusual that *she* didn't have to worry about it. But I knew that wasn't the truth, and I knew Hannah knew it, too. Although her question seemed simple, it landed as a single drop on the mirrored surface of a much deeper pond. Hannah wasn't really asking me if children ever died. She was asking if I was willing to admit that *she* might die, wondering if she was the only one who knew, if I was willing to know it, too.

"Yes, Hannah, sometimes children die," I said quietly.

Another drop in the pond. A question rolled off my tongue before I had a chance to think about it.

"Do you know what happens when they die?" I asked.

Silence; without breath.

"Uh-huh," she said. "They go to heaven and keep God company." She gripped my hand tighter and hopped like a bunny onto the sidewalk.

TRUTH IS FIERCE and unrelenting. We cannot change it, but we *can* change the way we live with it. Making mistakes, not being loved, and dying are inescapable experiences of being human; so is our fear of them. By facing those fears, we have a chance to step beyond them. When we are willing to do the best we can with what we know, to be honest with ourselves and others about who we are and what really matters to us, only then are the lives we live and the love we receive truly our own.

Joy

*finding it in the
darkest places*

He who hesitates before each step
will spend a lifetime on one foot.

—Chinese proverb

Hannah's Birthday

◆

I STOOD IN THE KITCHEN AND LISTENED TO THE SOUNDS OF laughter coming from the other room. I felt so relieved, I wanted to cry. In the month since Hannah's diagnosis, I had looked forward to this day with an impossible combination of anxiety and joy, haunted by one question: Was this going to be Hannah's third birthday or her last? I had agonized over whether to keep it simple or to plan something more elaborate in case she might never have another. When I asked Hannah how she wanted to celebrate the day, she had said, "I want a party with a Little Mermaid cake, not too much people and not too much gifts."

"What if you could do anything you wanted," I asked, "like going to see *Sesame Street Live* and inviting all your friends?"

"No, Mommy," she said. "I want a party with a Little Mermaid cake, not too much people and not too much gifts."

Rummaging through a drawer for the package of birthday candles, I could hear the children giggling and chattering. They were still breathless from their backyard treasure hunt. Each of them was a vision of loveliness in "discovered" finery: rhinestone tiaras, gold bangle bracelets, and plastic bead necklaces. Earlier, they had transformed a pile of wooden dowels, iridescent ribbons, glitter, and glue into magic wands that they were now using to bop each other on the head.

A quieter hum came from the mothers who were standing in one corner, sipping mugs of coffee. Deep in conversation, they paused occasionally to cast disapproving glances at wand-wielding treasure hunters whose behavior threatened to get out of hand. The ordinariness of it all was a relief from the initial awkwardness everyone had felt. The children had greeted Hannah shyly, tentatively. It was clear they had been reminded just before coming that Hannah had had surgery and might still feel sick. The mothers had embraced me with the same sort of shyness, as if they were uncertain whether to offer congratulations or condolences. I was sympathetic; even *I* wasn't sure if I wanted to smile or burst into tears.

Hannah had been the one to step into the moment and set us all straight.

"Hey, you guys, do you want to see my scar?" she asked, reaching for the hem of her dress.

"You mean you can show it to us?" her friend Jackie whispered, wide-eyed and incredulous.

"Of course!" Hannah responded. "It's just surgery."

She lifted and tucked the hem of her dress under her chin, exposing a whip of angry-red, still-stapled flesh that cut from one side of her abdomen to the other. The kids, instinctively curious, crowded close and responded with appreciative ooooʼs and aaahhhhʼs.

One of the mothers turned to me and whispered, "Is this okay with you?"

I smiled and shrugged my shoulders. "If itʼs okay with her, itʼs okay with me."

"Does it hurt?" one of the children asked.

"Not so much," Hannah answered. "My doctors gave me medicine and pizza, so I got better much faster."

"Wow, I want to have surgery!" someone else said. The others nodded in agreement.

There was a slight pause, and then Jackie asked, "Hannah, can you still play?"

"Of course, you silly," Hannah said. "This is a party, isnʼt it?"

Everyone laughed. The awkward spell had been broken and the party had begun.

I found the packet of birthday candles in the drawer, removed three of them, and slid them into one corner of the cake. I stepped back and smiled. This was no supermarket bakeshop cake; it was a masterpiece that Hannah and I had created together. On it, plastic figures of the Little Mermaid and Prince Eric stood, holding hands, on a brown-frosted island in the middle of a blue-and-green frosted sea. Here and there, holes the size of Hannahʼs index finger were outlined in chocolate cake crumbs, where Hannah had "tested" to make sure all the frostings tasted the same.

I lit the candles. They seemed dwarfed by the large cake. Three wasn't enough candles for a cake or enough years for a life. Tears I had been holding inside welled up. I blinked hard. I couldn't cry now. I would ruin the happiest moment of the whole day. Taking a deep breath, I picked up the cake, pasted a smile on my face, and stepped into the dining room. "Happy birthday to you . . ." The laughter and talking stopped as everyone joined in. I maneuvered the cake through an obstacle course of children, balloons, and tissue paper streamers, so engrossed in getting the cake to the table without igniting anyone or anything, that I didn't notice what Hannah was doing. When I finally looked up, my pasted-on grin slid off my chin.

Unlike everyone around her, Hannah wasn't smiling. She was solemn, quiet, almost completely still. Only her head moved as her eyes traveled slowly from one person to the next, resting finally on me. For a split second, I thought something was wrong; she was tired or sad, or the excitement was too much for her. Then I realized, far from feeling unhappy, Hannah was letting everyone and everything in this moment seep into her heart. As the loud, off-key rendition of "Happy Birthday" came to an end, bright eyes and flushed faces turned to look at her. She smiled slightly, still taking it all in. Everyone waited. A long silence. The other children began to wriggle impatiently.

"Make a wish, Hannah," someone called out.

Hannah looked at me. Her eyes burned into my heart. The adults were no longer smiling. The kids were no longer wriggling. Everyone was watching Hannah;

Hannah was watching me. The room was suspended in a hush, like the fullness in church after the last "amen." Finally, finally, with only a whisper of breath, Hannah blew the flames out. Even as she did it, her eyes never left mine. I felt more present, more *there* with her than I had felt with any other person, ever.

In one breath, Hannah blew out her candles and blew open my heart. I now knew there was a joy beyond happiness, out-loud laughs, and pasted-on grins. Its essence was stillness; a deep quiet that could be inhaled, that poured through my body until there was no part that was not filled.

Anticipation

I WANTED TO BOW LOW, DIG A HOLE, AND BURY MYSELF IN gratitude. I would have if I had been able to take my eyes off Hannah. She was waving to me from the school bus window, the pink baseball cap on her head knocked sideways in the hustle to find her seat.

Since the day Dr. Kamalaker had told us Hannah had a cancer no one was sure how to treat, Claude and I had begun living the paradox of wanting to do anything to find a cure and needing to preserve the quality of time Hannah had left. Claude had spent hours on the Internet and the phone, talking to doctors and medical librarians across the country, amassing a notebook, five inches thick, of every piece of information he could find about Hannah's cancer. Some part of him seemed convinced that Hannah's illness was like a particularly difficult engineering problem; if he just had the right information, he'd be able to figure it out.

One of the first things we realized was that because the cancer was so aggressive and rare, the treatments were, too. We used Dr. Markoff's rule and made the best decisions we could with the information we had at the time. After meeting personally with doctors in New York and Philadelphia, and speaking with others on the phone, Claude and I had agreed to try the chemotherapy protocol used on the little girl in Washington State who was still alive fifteen months after her diagnosis. The chemotherapy would be administered once a week at the outpatient clinic, which was only twenty minutes from home. We trusted Dr. Kamalaker and Dr. Bekele and appreciated how gracefully Jill, the social worker, had eased herself into our lives.

It was Jill who had broken the news to me that Hannah wouldn't be able to go to preschool. She and I were sitting beside Hannah's bed just after her surgery.

"I understand you're making arrangements for Hannah to start preschool next month," she said. She cleared her throat and shifted in her chair. "You realize, don't you, that chemotherapy will severely compromise Hannah's immune system. Preschool," she continued, laying a hand lightly on my arm, "is definitely out of the question."

I had taken a moment to let her words sink in. I knew that what she said was true. But to me, Hannah was a three-year-old first, and a cancer patient second.

"You don't understand," I said. "After everything Hannah's been through, I won't take preschool away from her. You see, she wants to ride on a bus and go on field trips with her friends. I'm willing to do anything to make that happen."

Jill wasn't giving up. "People will do amazing things to help kids in Hannah's situation. I'm sure we can arrange for a school bus, an empty one, to come to your house and take her for a ride. Hannah won't know the difference."

I laughed and shook my head. If ever I was going to be right about something, it was this. "Jill, I'm sure you know a lot of things, but if you think an empty school bus pulling up to the house is going to fool Hannah, you definitely don't know *her*."

Hannah started preschool the week after her third birthday. Once the decision was made, everyone committed themselves to making it work. Mrs. Fisher and Mrs. Forsythe, Hannah's teachers, met with nurses from the clinic to discuss ways to minimize Hannah's exposure to germs. They also met with the parents of the other children in the class to address any concerns or questions they had. Ursula, the clinic's receptionist, scheduled all Hannah's tests and chemotherapy appointments so as not to interfere with her Tuesday/Thursday morning class. Hannah threw herself wholeheartedly into school. As a result, her treatment became simply one more thing on our calendar, rather than the only thing on our minds.

Mrs. Fisher nudged the last of her charges up the steps of the bus, counting each head as they passed.

"Okay, moms," she called out. "It looks like we're ready to roll!"

Her announcement was greeted with a chorus of shouts from twenty-nine three- and four-year-olds. The bus driver slid the doors shut and started the engine. Through the window, I saw Hannah grab the back of the seat in front of her and bounce up and down, a huge grin on her face. As the bus began to pull away, she let go briefly, turned, and waved. At that moment I snapped my camera and snatched a memory that, to this day, sits in a silver frame on Jill's desk.

"Every morning," Jill told me, "Hannah waves to me from the window of that bus, and reminds me that more things are possible than I know."

No Worries

❧

I WAS UNLOADING THE DISHWASHER WHEN HANNAH DANCED into the kitchen. She was wearing her glitter-pink bathing suit and waving her birthday magic wand.

"Mommy, let's finger-paint," she said, pirouetting around the table. "Pleeeeze," she added.

I straightened up, arching the aches out of my back. Last night's dishes were stacked, unwashed, on piles of unopened mail on the counter. The message light was blinking on the phone-answering machine, and the buzzer on the clothes dryer was reminding me every two minutes that it was ready for more. I had an endless list of things to do, and finger-painting wasn't one of them.

No matter. We stood the big, blue easel in a warm patch of September sun in the thick backyard grass. Then we took off our shoes and slid glossy white sheets of finger-paint paper under the bright-yellow clip. Hannah arranged cups of paint in the tray beneath; strawberry red, ocean blue, lemon-drop yellow, new-tomato green.

We dipped our fingers in the cups and smooshed them around.

"Gross!" Hannah said.

Giggling, we lifted them out. Thick, gooey globs of paint dropped off our fingertips into the grass. We smudged the paper with color in looping, rainbow swirls. We created one masterpiece after the next. Half an hour later, Will came home from school. Seeing us, he grinned and dropped his backpack on the ground, and he, too, became a dancing, painting fool.

Later that night, I sat at the kitchen table with a luke-warm cup of coffee, studying the paintings taped to the cupboard doors. They were beautiful. I was actually *proud* of mine. A knot in my heart began to unravel. For years I had been wanting to paint and had told myself I would have to take lessons first, so I wouldn't do it wrong. Today, without brushes and palettes to intimidate me, my fear had literally slipped through my fingers. I had lost myself in the joy of it.

Swirling my coffee around in its mug, I watched the moon rise through the kitchen window. I could feel a whole other life beating beneath my skin.

The Unbirthday

"MOMMY, WHY AM I NOT GOING TO HAVE A BIRTHDAY after four?"

We had gone to the grocery store. Hannah's question dropped into the car just as I turned into our driveway. Memories of her third birthday and our conversation about whether children ever die were as fresh in me as the scar from her surgery. She sounded perplexed but certain; as if she knew it was true, but didn't quite understand why.

I pulled the car into the garage, shifted the gear into park, and turned off the ignition. I looked in the rearview mirror; Hannah was watching the back of my head. I took a deep breath and turned to face her.

"I'm not sure that's true, Hannah," I offered, hating the exaggerated cheerfulness in my voice. "After your fourth birthday, you'll have your fifth birthday."

She looked at me suspiciously. I suddenly felt self-conscious.

"Are you sure?" she asked.

"Well . . ." I hesitated. "The doctors are doing everything they can to help your body get better so you can have *lots* more birthdays."

She cocked her head and smiled at me sympathetically.

"Well, I'm not going to," she said; not challenging me, simply telling me.

As I reached over to unbuckle her car seat, I knew she was already so far ahead of me, I could only pray to keep up. I couldn't help wondering, too, what else she knew.

Drug Dealing at the Y

*

HANNAH AND I WERE SCRUNCHED INTO A CURTAINED dressing room at the Y. I was trying not to hurry, but I also didn't want to keep Claude and Will waiting any longer than necessary. She and I were both naked, having just peeled wet bathing suits off our bodies. Hannah was giggling because the towel I had wrapped around her head like a turban kept sliding over her eyes. She was sitting on a wooden bench against the wall. I was kneeling in a puddle on the floor in front of her. Next to her, on the bench, was a scattered collection of medical paraphernalia in sterile bubble packs.

As part of her treatment protocol, a Broviac catheter had been implanted in Hannah's chest to give doctors a direct line into her bloodstream. Its tubes needed to be flushed several times a day and the site kept as clean and sterile as possible.

Dr. Kamalaker had designated me the sole person responsible for handling and maintaining the Broviac and its site; even nurses and residents were given instructions not to touch it. He explained that the risk of complications was greatly reduced if the Broviac was handled exclusively by one person; his decision had also validated me as a respected member of the medical team. That wasn't the only unusual step he had been willing to take; the fact that Hannah and I were dripping wet and giggling in the dressing room of the Y was a testament to his humanity and imagination.

There was almost nothing Hannah loved more than swimming. She would stand at the edge of the pool, bend her knees, swing her arms back and forth, count "one, two, three, GO!" and leap into Claude's waiting arms. The bigger the splash the better. She'd bob to the surface with the help of the bright orange bubble strapped to her back, paddle to the side, squirm over the edge, and do it again. We would tire of the game long before she did. "Just one more time, Daddy," she'd plead.

That's what we had told Dr. Kamalaker when we insisted that Hannah had to be able to swim. Dr. Kamalaker had considerable doubts; without question, the public pool was a breeding ground for germs. I had explained to him that I didn't want to expose Hannah to unnecessary risks, but I wasn't willing to postpone her joy, either. It seemed a greater risk to think she might never swim again than it did to think she might get an infection from it.

Dr. Kamalaker listened quietly and then stared out the window. Finally he stood up, opened the door to the supply cabinet, and rummaged around. Thirty seconds later he emerged with a satisfied grin and a box of waterproof patches.

"You can use these," he said. "Also, clean and flush her caps, tube, and site before and after she swims. We'll try it a few times, and if she manages to do it without getting an infection, you can continue indefinitely with my blessing."

Now I pulled the disposable rubber gloves over my hands with a loud snap. Hannah grabbed another one and handed it to me.

"Make me a bunny, Mom," she begged.

"Okay, just one," I agreed. I scrunched the wrist of the glove between my thumb and forefinger, held it to my mouth, and blew. The powdery latex tasted bitter on my lips. The glove's fingers and thumb swelled up, and then the rest of it did, too. Now came the part that separated the experts from the novices: I clamped my thumb and finger together to keep the air from escaping and wrestled a knot into the remaining latex. Hannah squealed and kissed me.

"Thanks, Mom!"

"You're welcome, Missy." I smiled. "Now, let's get this Broviac flushed."

While I filled two syringes, one with heparin, one with saline, Hannah tore open four packages of alcohol wipes and set them carefully on the bench. Then she lifted the tubes of the Broviac, keeping her hands clear of the ends. I rubbed the end caps with alcohol and reached for the first syringe. Raising it above my head in order to see it in a brighter light, I flicked the syringe with my finger to force any air bubbles into the tip. Then, just as I depressed the plunger to expel the excess air, the curtain slid open.

A woman in a blue-flowered bathing suit held the edge

of the curtain in her hand. Her eyes widened and moved slowly, from the sight of the gauze pads and vials on the bench, to Hannah and her Broviac, to my rubber gloves and the syringe in my hand. Without a word, she slid the curtain shut. We saw her daisy-trimmed flip-flops take a step back and pause. Then they turned and slapped across the floor, until they reached the door. I heard it open and shut. I turned to Hannah.

She was grinning mischievously.

"Mommy," Hannah said, "that lady was really surprised! Do you think it's because she never saw naked people before?"

Inhale

I WROTE ONE LINE IN MY JOURNAL.

"A dark day."

The tumor was back. The doctors had seen it on a routine X-ray. Despite eight weeks of chemotherapy, microscopic cells from the original mass had migrated and multiplied into a dark spot on Hannah's lower left lung. The scar from her surgery had barely healed.

Claude and I were faced with an agonizing decision. If we did nothing, Hannah might be dead before Christmas. We weren't ready. Using Dr. Markoff's rule, we scheduled a second surgery to remove the tumor, and made plans for Hannah to undergo an autologous bone marrow transplant. Although there were other experimental therapies available, most of them would almost certainly require Hannah to spend whatever time she had left in a hospital. We weren't willing to subject her to that. We decided that the transplant offered a balance between risk and hope that we could live with. We also decided that if Hannah relapsed again, we'd have to let her go.

The release forms Claude and I had to sign stated the paradox perfectly: The treatment she was about to undergo could not be expected to cure her, and it might kill her. Even if by some miracle she were to live into adolescence, she'd be unable to enter puberty without medical intervention, and she would never bear children.

One doctor we consulted had summed it up in a sentence: "If I were you, I'd pray she stays healthy long enough for these things to be a problem."

The day before her surgery, as Hannah and I walked to the park, I wasn't thinking about any of this. It was a sweater-weather kind of day: warm afternoon sun, crisp autumn breeze, and a golden maple underfoot crunch. I felt the warmth of her fingers wrapped around mine and heard the lilt and pitch of her voice as she made plans to wear a princess costume to the hospital. The purple pom-pom on her woolen cap bobbed up and down as she walked.

I inhaled the moment, savoring everything in it. There was nothing to do, or say, or wish for. I was lucky to be alive, and luckier still that Hannah was. I held my breath as long as I could, hoping that some feather of joy from this moment might lodge in my lungs today so it could drift lightly and unexpectedly into one of the dark moments I knew was ahead.

Magic

A WEEK AFTER HANNAH'S SECOND SURGERY, WE RETURNED home. Hannah performed two somersaults in the middle of the living room floor to celebrate. Too surprised to stop her, I had closed my eyes and winced.

Now, three days later, even *I* felt a million miles away from doctors, treatments, and cancer. Claude and I were splayed like rag dolls on upholstered chairs, grateful for the air-conditioning. Our luggage was a tumbled pile of leather and nylon on one of the double beds. Will and Hannah had wriggled their bodies through a split in the curtains and pressed their noses against the fourteenth-floor window.

"Look, Will," Hannah screamed. "I can see Cinderella's castle! I hope she's home!"

"Of course she's not home, Hannah; she's not real," Will explained, somewhat impatiently.

"She is too, Will. You'll see." Hannah sniffed.

"Come on, Mom and Dad," Will said. "We can't wait."

Claude and I looked at each other and laughed. The

alarm clock had buzzed us awake at four-thirty A.M. in New Jersey. A stretch limousine had picked us up half an hour later and deposited us at the airline terminal before six. Will and Hannah had slept through the flight to Orlando. A friendly couple had met us at the gate, walked us to our rental car, and pinned a badge on Hannah that identified her as a Make-A-Wish kid. We had checked into our hotel before noon.

Hannah's relapse had officially qualified her for an all-expenses-paid trip to Walt Disney World. The vacation was a welcome and generous respite, but any relief we felt was temporary: Hannah's bone marrow aspiration had already been scheduled for the following week.

Claude and I hauled our bodies into standing position.

"Yippee!" Will and Hannah cried.

We rode the monorail to the Magic Kingdom. Cinderella's castle was our first stop. As we crossed the moat, walked beneath the turreted entrance, and stepped into the shade of the tiled mosaic reception hall, I felt drawn into the magic of happily-ever-after. My mind knew it wasn't real, but my heart was grateful. I could hear the hum of excited voices and clatter of pewter dishes spilling out of the doors of the banquet hall at the other end. Most of the people around us headed there, including Claude, who wanted to see if we could get a table without reservations. Will and Hannah hung back, staring transfixed at the suits of armor and crests lining the walls. Suddenly, Hannah froze. A slight figure in a long blue gown with a twist of golden hair looped behind a jeweled tiara had stepped quietly out of an alcove in front of her. Will's jaw dropped.

"Cinderella," he whispered.

Cinderella kneeled in front of Hannah.

"Hello, I'm Cinderella," she said softly. "What's your name?"

Hannah hadn't moved. Her eyes traveled from the crown on Cinderella's head, over her smiling face, down her billowing skirt to the clear glasslike slipper just visible beneath the hem.

"My name's Hannah," she said finally. "And that's my brother, Will," she added, pointing to him. She paused, leaned toward Cinderella, and in a loud whisper said, "He didn't know you were real, but *I* did."

Will squirmed and rolled his eyes. Cinderella gave him a wink.

"That's okay, Will," Cinderella said. He smiled bashfully, clearly relieved.

Cinderella turned her attention back to Hannah.

"How are you, Hannah?" she asked.

"I just had surgery," Hannah said quietly. "Do you want to see my scar?"

I suspected Cinderella had already noticed Hannah's Make-A-Wish button.

"Okay," she said softly.

Hannah slowly raised her dress. Cinderella looked at Hannah's belly and then, without a word, opened her arms. Hannah threw herself into Cinderella's embrace. As she held Hannah, the young woman looked at me over Hannah's shoulder, her eyes full of tears.

"Thank you for sharing that with me, Hannah," she whispered.

Hannah loosened her grip and gave her a kiss.

"You're welcome," Hannah said.

Cinderella stood up, dabbed a finger under her mascaraed lashes, and straightened her skirt. Will stepped forward and extended his hand.

"It's nice to meet you, Cinderella," he said.

"It's nice to meet *you*, Will," Cinderella said, shaking his hand.

Hannah skipped breathlessly around the two of them.

"You see, Will," she cried, "I *told* you she was real."

"Yep, Hannah," he said, winking at Cinderella, "you were right."

As the three of us headed toward the banquet hall, I was grinning from ear to ear. It didn't matter that Cinderella was a girl from Iowa in a beautiful costume. The joy we had experienced in the meeting was real, and that was magic enough for me.

Secrets

WE HAD TAKEN A BREAK FROM THE AFTERNOON SUN AND the crush of sunburned tourists. Will and Hannah sat cross-legged on the floor, watching Disney cartoons. Claude's eyes were already closed. Stretched out next to him, exhausted but content, I ran my hand over my belly. There was new life in me. The day before we left for Florida, I had seen the white pad on the pregnancy test stick split in two by a thin line that deepened from robin's-egg to deep-sea blue. Claude and I had embraced and cried. It felt good and different from any of my previous pregnancies. There was no wild elation; only a quiet contentment and surrender. This pregnancy, I knew, was up to God; it wasn't up to me.

We had decided not to tell anyone, not even the kids. If I was still pregnant at Christmas, having passed the critical eight-week mark, we would share the news then.

I closed my eyes and was almost asleep when I felt a small hand shaking my shoulder.

"Mommy," Hannah whispered loudly in my ear, "are you awake?"

I lifted my heavy eyelids and blinked a few times.

"Yes, Missy. What is it?"

"Mommy, I want to tell you something about the baby who died," she answered.

"Which baby?" I asked, sliding over and motioning for her to join me on the bed.

Hannah snuggled close, nestling her head under my chin.

"You know, the baby that was in your tummy; the one who wasn't strong enough to be born," she said. I nodded.

"Well," she said excitedly, placing one hand on my stomach and looking into my eyes. "you don't have to feel sad about it, because God's already making us a *new* baby."

I opened and closed my mouth; I didn't know what to say. Either she was guessing, in which case I would have to lie to keep from spilling the beans, or she knew, in which case I wouldn't know what to say anyway.

I decided, as she sat there grinning at me, that I would have to let it go; it was simply one more thing that I would never know.

Christmas Presence

A LIGHT SNOW WAS FALLING OUTSIDE, JUST IN TIME FOR Christmas Day. A tiny artificial tree, hung with miniature ornaments and lights, sat in one corner of the hospital room next to stacks of books, puzzles, stuffed animals, and a Barbie doll. All the windows were covered with stick-on holiday decals of stockings, candy canes, and stars. A chain of red and green construction paper was draped from one end of the room to the other.

It seemed that Bethlehem's grace had made it to our neck of the woods; Hannah was still alive, and the baby inside me was, too.

For the past three weeks, Hannah and I had been in isolation from germs and the world in a ten-by-twelve-foot room. Although this hospital was more than an hour and a half's drive from our house, it was the only one in our area with the facility to perform bone marrow transplants that had agreed to let me be with Hannah twenty-four hours a day. Insisting that I be allowed to stay with her was one of the best decisions Claude and I ever made.

For ten days, doctors had pumped Hannah's body full of chemotherapy drugs, in an attempt to destroy any cancer cells that remained. The bags of chemicals were covered with fluorescent orange warning stickers that read "Danger," "Toxic Chemicals," "Hazardous Waste." After hanging them on Hannah's IV pole, the nurses checked, double-checked, and triple-checked their clipboards before starting the drip. I recorded everything in a small notebook Claude had given me. He had lined it with rows of narrow columns to record the date, time, name, and dosage of every medication Hannah received. It became, in an odd sort of way, a journal of the last year of Hannah's life.

As soon as one bag was empty, another was hung in its place. Almost immediately, Hannah's body had begun to deteriorate, and I began to believe that Claude and I had made the gravest mistake of our lives. The chemicals made Hannah sick to her stomach and burned her mouth, throat, and intestinal tract. Her hair fell out in handfuls; only a few wisps stubbornly clung to her bald head. Every inch of her skin was covered with a raw, bumpy rash. Beneath the rash, her flesh turned the color of pollen.

In an attempt to minimize bedsores and infection, the doctors ordered me to bathe her five times a day in a blue plastic tub the nurses set up in the middle of the floor. Each time I lifted Hannah's limp, aching body off the bed, she whimpered and moaned. Several times I quietly rebelled against the insanity of it all, lied to the nurses, and told them I had bathed her when I had actually let her sleep instead.

During the first week of treatment, I prayed every day that things wouldn't get worse, that Hannah's body could have a rest from the exhaustion and pain.

When the doctors reminded me that Hannah's white blood cell count would have to drop to almost zero before the chemotherapy could be stopped, and the closer she got to that goal, the sicker she would become, I began to pray for her to be sick, sick enough for the madness to stop.

Finally, when the light had almost faded from her eyes, the chemotherapy bags were taken down, and bags of her own bone marrow, harvested earlier, were pumped through the Broviac into her veins. The room filled with a choking odor that sweated out of Hannah's feverish body, a combination of chemotherapy agents and bone marrow preservative. The smell burned my lungs and nostrils, making it difficult to breathe without feeling sick. I now knew what the valley of the shadow of death smelled like: fermented tomato juice.

For days Hannah lay in bed, still as death, barely able to sip water from a straw. The nurses drew blood from her every four hours to make sure her white cell count was continuing to rise. Each time, I held my breath. Slowly, as Hannah's cells began to regenerate, I transitioned from praying that she would live until Christmas to praying that her counts would be high enough to allow visitors. It was a race to the finish. The numbers climbed steadily for a week, and then, three days before Christmas, they stalled, dropped, and refused to budge. Two days before Christmas, the nurse on the afternoon shift took an extra, unscheduled sample of

Hannah's blood, hoping for the best. Her hunch paid off. It was as if someone in our room had won the lottery; doctors, nurses, even the floor mopper had knocked on the window and signaled a "thumbs-up."

Now Hannah was a vision of loveliness, kneeling on her bed in front of the dollhouse she had received from Santa. She was wearing a lace headband around her bald head and a new ivory satin dress that would have been perfect for the flower girl at a Mafia wedding. That is why I had known she would love it.

The night before, on Christmas Eve, Claude had come to stay with her so I could run out and buy a few last-minute gifts. It was the first time I had stepped out of the hospital in three weeks. As I had stood in a store at the mall, holding up the Mafia Christmas dress, a woman browsing through a rack of little boys' trousers noticed.

"Are you thinking of buying that dress?" she asked.

"Well, yes, but it's pretty expensive," I said sheepishly.

The woman smiled. "I have three boys," she said emphatically. "BUY THAT DRESS!"

Now, looking at Hannah, I was glad I had. It was the first time she had worn anything besides a hospital gown in two and a half weeks. She had even buzzed the nurses' station and told them to come to see. Compared to how she had looked days before, she looked positively radiant. Although her face and arms were bloated from having so many fluids passing through her and her eyes looked dull and sleepy, she was sitting up. Her skin was less yellow, and only lightly speckled from the residue of her rash.

Claude, Will, and I grinned at each other from behind our paper masks. The three of us were also wearing plastic shower caps, long-sleeved hospital gowns, rubber gloves, and elastic-edged booties. The masks constantly slipped off our noses no matter how creatively we tied them behind our heads. Hannah called the outfits "space suits." Everyone, except her, had to wear one. Her immune system was still so compromised that the slightest infection could kill her.

It felt so good to be together. I felt as if my cup was running over. Everything that would have seemed ordinary a month ago now seemed as miraculous as a resurrection. Claude seemed to think so, too. He was hopping forward and backward, tipping his camera, snapping pictures.

"I can't wait to show everyone how great she looks," Claude said.

"Hey, you two," I said to Will and Hannah, "Daddy and I have some news to share with you."

The two of them looked up. Claude reached for my hand and squeezed.

"Our family is going to have a new baby."

"When?" Will and Hannah cried in unison.

"In July," Claude said.

The two of them squealed and hugged each other.

"Wow," said Will, "this is the best Christmas present ever. Hannah, don't you think it would be really cool if it's a baby brother?"

Hannah frowned. "I don't think that will work, Will," she said. "I want to name him Briar Rose, so he *has* to be a girl."

"Well, if his name is Briar Rose, *I* hope he's a girl, too," Will said.

While Claude continued to take more pictures, I let my eyes and heart be filled with all the joy in the room. What we were sharing could never be captured on the surface of a glossy photograph. This joy didn't need to be documented; it already had a permanent home in our hearts.

Communion with
Dr. Tomato-head

~

ABOUT A WEEK AFTER CHRISTMAS, HANNAH'S TRANSPLANT
doctor entered her room with big news.

"You can have anything you want to eat for dinner
tonight, Hannah-banana," Dr. Tomato-head said.

Dr. Tomato-head's real name was Dr. Brockstein.
Hannah had started calling him Dr. Tomato-head when he
insisted on calling her Hannah-banana.

He was obviously pleased with his generous offer.
Hannah looked at him thoughtfully. She was wearing her
Christmas dress with her red shoes.

"It's true, Hannah," I said. "Your body has worked really
hard to get strong enough for you to be able to eat again.
You can have anything you want."

She screwed up her face and tapped the side of her head
with her finger.

"Hmmm . . ." she said, closing her eyes to think. "Do
you have any hard rolls?" she asked.

The doctor and I looked at each other, surprised.

"I think we do," he said, "and if we don't, we'll get some."

"Thank you," Hannah said, folding her hands in her lap.

"Is that *all* you want?" he asked.

"No, actually, there's one more thing," Hannah said. Dr. Tomato-head's face brightened with obvious relief.

"I would like some grape juice, too, please."

"Are you sure that's all?" he asked, his brow slightly wrinkled in confusion. "You could have pizza, ice cream, chocolate chip cookies . . . *anything!*"

Hannah peered at him, slightly annoyed now.

"I want a hard roll and grape juice," she said, holding her hands out, palm side up in exasperation, *"like Communion at church,"* she added, as if it were so obvious that we were dolts for not seeing it.

She turned to me. "Mom, will you help me take off my dress? I don't want to spill juice on it."

Ten minutes later, Dr. Tomato-head, two nurses, and I watched as Hannah slowly and thoughtfully tore the roll into pieces and dipped each one into the glass of grape juice before putting it in her mouth. Oblivious to us, she chewed, swallowed, and stared silently into the slip of twilight sky outside her window. I wanted to kneel in front of her and kiss her feet.

Two hours later, she rang the nurses and asked for sliced tomatoes with mustard.

Change of Mind,
Change of Heart

HANNAH'S HEAD WAS NOW COMPLETELY BALD; THE LAST
few wisps of hair had finally dropped off. We had been in
the transplant unit for four and a half weeks. Both of us had
had enough; we were more than ready to go home.

I handed her a red plastic cup, filled with apple juice.
She took a sip.

"Nope, it's not right," she said, handing it back to me.

I couldn't believe it. I had been doing it, at her request,
the same way for days: apple juice in the red cup, milk in
the green, Pepsi in the yellow, and water in the blue.

"It's not right," she repeated, looking evenly at me.

"Which one isn't right?" I asked.

"All of them," she said.

I wanted to throw the whole lot against the wall. I
breathed slowly and counted to ten. Usually, it was my
greatest joy to let Hannah decide which beverage she
wanted in each cup. While some people seemed concerned
that I might be spoiling her, I didn't agree. I saw it as a way
to preserve some sense of Hannah's dignity. So many things

were literally being forced down her throat, she needed to have control over something. Today, though, I felt more exhausted than willing.

"Hannah, this is exactly the way you've asked me to do it every other day."

"I know," she said, folding her hands on her lap, "but today," she paused, and leaned forward, drawing her words out as if she were speaking to a particularly thick-headed child, *"I changed my mind."*

My exasperation melted away as I threw my head back and laughed. She had said it as if changing one's mind and running the risk of pissing someone off was a new concept to me. She was right; it was.

Savage Joy

NOW THAT HER COUNTS WERE HIGH ENOUGH, HANNAH WAS allowed to venture out of her room. No longer content to stroll or wander, what she loved most these days was speed.

"Let's go for a ride," Hannah said.

We pulled her bike from its parking spot under the anteroom sink and pushed it into the center of the hall. The two-wheeler was hot pink and purple and sported a pair of training wheels. The Make-A-Wish Foundation had left it for her on Christmas Eve. Hannah stuffed her pink blanket into the basket on the front and climbed onto the seat. I gave her a slight push. Stretching her legs as far as they could reach, she began to pedal. As she picked up speed on the linoleum floor, I ran along beside her, the IV pole careening. The bike rocked from side to side, its sparkling handlebar streamers flying.

"Hang on, Hannah," I shrieked as she lifted both hands to wave to the nurses at the nurses' station, who grinned and waved as we passed.

"You're going to wear your mom out, Hannah!" one of them cried.

Hannah threw her head back and laughed. I laughed, too. It was more joy than I could fit in my heart to see her having so much fun.

"Look out below!" she shouted as we rounded the corner by the elevators. She coasted to a stop and hopped off her bike to turn it around. As I untangled and readjusted the IV tubes for the return lap, I noticed a small crowd of people weeping and whispering outside a rarely used room at the end of the hall.

"What's happening down there?" I asked a nurse who had broken away from the group and walked toward me.

"The little boy in that room was hit by a car this morning and just died," she said softly.

I felt as if I had been punched in the stomach and, at the same time, lucky in a way that I would have hated to admit out loud. I couldn't imagine losing Hannah to death so suddenly and unexpectedly, without time to prepare her or myself for what was coming, without a chance to savor every last drop of her before she was gone. Had this boy's parents even had a chance to say good-bye?

No matter how intense and frightening the months since Hannah's diagnosis had been, I felt grateful for every moment I had shared with her. Even the darkest ones had contained slivers of savage joy. I now knew that there was something simple yet exquisite about the gift of time; time to savor, time to remember, time to say good-bye.

Nurse Katie and the Tea Party

꙳

HANNAH AND I CAME HOME THE FIRST WEEK IN JANUARY. She returned to preschool a week later, wearing her Christmas dress and a black velvet hat with a garish pink bow that kept slipping off her bald head and knocking the paper hospital mask off her nose. Her friends at school had exclaimed over her dress and hardly seemed to notice her lack of hair.

Today, Hannah was wearing her Christmas dress again, because, as she had explained to me, "this is a very, very *special* occasion." Nurse Katie was coming for tea.

Katie was one of Hannah's favorite nurses; she worked at the hospital where Hannah had her surgeries. In her early twenties, barely five feet tall, with short dark hair and dancing eyes, Katie had never seemed distracted by something else when she was with Hannah. She always seemed to genuinely care how Hannah was doing, and was never too busy to be silly.

The two of them used to play their favorite game every time Katie came into Hannah's hospital room.

"Is there anything I can get for you, little Miss Hannah?" Katie would begin, trying to look as serious as she could. Hannah would grin and fold her hands in her lap.

"Yes, there is," she would say, barely able to finish the sentence before she burst out laughing. "Nurse Katie, could I please have a tomatie?"

Katie would lean toward Hannah and, in a solemn, serious voice, say, "I'm so sorry, ma'am, but the Katies have eaten all the tomaties, although we still have plenty of bananas for little Miss Hannahs."

Now, Hannah was setting the tea party table herself. Walking slowly and carefully, she carried an eclectic assortment of china plates and cups, one at a time, from the kitchen to the coffee table in the living room. She ordered the cups and plates into a lopsided circle and set a white plastic daisy and vase from her Barbie tea set in the center. Three leftover birthday napkins, a Winnie-the-Pooh and two Little Mermaids, were joined by one that said "Happy New Year," lined up end to end "so we can see the pictures on them," Hannah explained.

She had decided we should pour the tea from the "grown-ups'" pot. The one from her Barbie set was already stuffed with an impressive collection of Band-Aids. Because we used so many of them, we had become aficionados. Buying anything but the "regular" ones, we now had boxes of them in every size, pattern, and color.

As I watched Hannah arrange and rearrange the items on the table, I held myself back from making any suggestions. It wasn't easy. There was a part of me, I realized, that

was overly critical of everything, that wanted to teach people, especially my children, about the "right" way to do
things.

Hannah was smiling and humming, every once in a
while stepping back to survey her work. She was in no
hurry, and seemed completely unconcerned about the way
a tea party is "supposed" to look. I watched her quietly,
savoring the joy she was experiencing and the care she was
giving to everything that she was doing. I longed to bring
the same attention to the busy-ness in *my* every day, to do
something simply for the joy of doing it, without worrying
whether people noticed or liked it.

Joy, I realized then, is not concerned about being messy,
mismatched, or unloved. If I was serious about living life
more fully, I was going to have to let go of my need for
everything, including myself and others, to be perfect.

Joy in a Jeep

🖋

I HAD TAKEN DOWN THE CURTAINS AND OPENED ALL THE windows, letting the warm spring breeze chase winter's mustiness out of the house. Claude was outside, raking and seeding the yard. Will and Hannah were helping me wipe woodwork and furniture with slippery lemon oil. We made our way through the downstairs and had just started on Will's room when I heard a vehicle pull into our driveway, its horn honking loudly. I didn't even have to look to know who it was. The kids didn't, either.

"Pastor LJ," they screamed, running to the window.

I heard Laurajane's laugh and got to the window just in time to see her blowing kisses from the front seat of her topless, bright red jeep.

"Hey, that looks cool," Will said, leaning dangerously out the window.

"It *is* cool." Laurajane laughed. She lifted her Phillies cap off her head. "Hey, what are you guys doing? Can you go for a ride?"

"We're cleaning," Hannah said, holding her dust rag up for Laurajane to see.

"Cleaning???" Laurajane shrieked, as Will and Hannah laughed. "You tell your mom there is absolutely, positively no cleaning allowed on a beautiful day like this. You two get down here right away and tell your mom she'd better come, too!"

Will and Hannah dropped their cloths and flew down the stairs, throwing themselves into Laurajane's arms. Planting a loud kiss on each of their cheeks, she lifted them over the side of the jeep and buckled both of them in. As the four of us backed down the driveway, Laurajane beeped the horn. Claude paused, grinned, and waved.

The sun was high in the sky and warm on our faces. Laurajane stepped on the gas.

"Faster!" Hannah yelled from the backseat as the wind whipped through the open jeep.

Laurajane and I glanced at each other and grinned. Her eyes were bright and wild. I knew mine were, too. Laurajane stepped on the gas. The jeep shot forward. We all whooped with glee. This was the most fun I'd had in a long time.

"Hey, Mom!" Hannah screamed. "I can feel the wind in my hair!"

I spun around to look. Sure enough, I could see it for the first time in the bright sunlight. Hannah's bald head was now covered with the slightest brush of down, and every wisp of it was standing on end in the stiff breeze. Hannah ran her hands over her scalp.

"I have hair," she screamed. "I have hair!"

"Yahoo!" Will whooped, leaning across the seat to give her a hug.

I started to cry. Laurajane did, too.

I mouthed the words "Thank you, thank you."

She reached across the front seat and gave my hand a squeeze. As we hurtled around a bend, Hannah shrieked again.

"Pastor LJ, Mommy. That's where I'm going to live!"

I looked where she was pointing. There, on the corner, was the pinkest house I had ever seen; every inch of it was painted light rose, except for its deep maroon trim.

"Yuck, Hannah," Will yelled. "That house is totally pink!"

Hannah giggled and screamed in his ear. "I'm going to have a pink car with no top on it, too."

Will shook his head and rolled his eyes.

"Girls," he said.

Nothing Special

SUNSET LICKED LIGHT FROM THE SKY. IT HAD BEEN another warm spring day. The air smelled ripe and muddy. Claude and I held hands and walked while Will and Hannah ran ahead. I was now six months pregnant, and I could feel the baby shift and settle into the rhythm of my stride.

Will's friend David was in the driveway of his house, playing basketball with his dad. Alan and Claude had coached a Little League team together and sometimes played pickup games of basketball with other dads on Tuesday evenings. David's little brother Michael, who was a few months older than Hannah, was squatting in the front yard, poking a stick into the dirt. Will cupped his hands and shouted to David, who grinned and hurled a long pass to him. Will caught the ball, dribbled to the hoop, and missed. Hannah, meanwhile, found a stick and joined Michael in the dirt. Alan saw Claude and me and waved. By the time Claude and I reached them, Alan, ducking and wheeling around the two older boys, had faked a few misses of his own.

"I need some help here, buddy," he called out.

Claude laughed and joined in. MaryAnn, Alan's wife, poked her head out the front door.

"I was wondering what all the commotion was about," she said, grinning.

She motioned for me to join her on the front step.

"Hey, Michael," she shouted. "What are you two up to?"

"We're looking for bugs," Hannah said.

"And worms," Michael added.

"Yeah, and worms," Hannah said.

"Oh, great," MaryAnn said, rolling her eyes. "I guess that means a second bath for both of you tonight."

It was right then that it happened. It was such a strange and glorious thing that if I hadn't experienced it myself, I wouldn't have believed it was possible. *I forgot that Hannah was sick!*

I wasn't even aware of having forgotten. It was as if I had been sucked out of the story of cancer, treatment, worry, and death. Hannah was playing in the dirt, and I was visiting with a friend. It was a moment of nothing special, of nothing going on.

In a flash, whatever had sucked me up spit me out again. Even so, something felt different. Although I remembered now that Hannah was sick, some part of the stillness had remained.

Later, I sat on the front porch, in the residue of that stillness, peeling away the layers of night sky. I noticed first the moths, beating their powdery bodies against the bulb of the porch light, then bats, with aerial precision, whiffing past. Beyond the bats, the moon, with its huge, unblinking face, then the planets flickering and galaxies spinning on an endless carpet of stars.

Listening to the night, I felt poised on the edge of greatness, certain that the silence I was feeling was God.

Celebrate

✦

I HEARD HANNAH PADDING UP THE STAIRS. I OPENED MY eyes and stretched. It was time to get up. I heard the shower running; Claude had managed to get out of bed without waking me. God bless him.

The door to our bedroom burst open.

"Mommy," Hannah cried, "isn't this a *great* day to be alive?"

She had stopped in the doorway, bright-eyed and beaming, her pink blanket dragging behind her. A puff of inch-long, fine blond hair stuck out every which way on her head. Her cheeks were full and pink. I noticed, for the first time, that the ruffled hem of her nightgown no longer pooled on the floor. I could see tiny, pink-polished toenails where it brushed the tops of her feet. As I smiled at her, she let go of the doorknob and her blanket, ran across the room, and flung herself onto the bed. Crawling toward me, she burrowed under the covers and nestled her head in the space between my neck and shoulder.

"Yes, Hannah," I said, burying my nose in her hair. "This *is* a great day to be alive."

JOY IS THE MAGIC and stillness that stand on the threshold of every moment, the experience of giving and living fully, without expecting anything in return. Because joy knows no rules, it isn't afraid to be imperfect, and it can surprise us even in the darkest places.

Faith

from "my will be done"
to "thy will be done"

Every time that we say 'Thy will be done,'
we should have in mind all possible
misfortunes added together.

—Simone Weil

Thy Will (and Mine) Be Done

IT WAS A GLORIOUS SPRING DAY, A WEEK BEFORE EASTER. Hannah and I had decided to walk to church. Will had ridden his bike ahead, and Claude, who had slept in, said he would join us later. Hannah and I held hands. Bulbs and buds, dormant all winter, were bursting into life. One magnolia tree, in particular, caught my eye. It was taller than the houses on either side; its branches, covered in enormous white-and-purple blooms, stretched upward, into forever.

"Mommy," Hannah said, pointing to it, "those are the flowers I'm going to have at my wedding!"

"They're beautiful, Hannah," I said, exhaling a prayer for it to be true. "Who are you going to marry?"

"Daddy, you silly." Hannah laughed.

These days, Hannah looked too healthy to be sick. She had already worn through her first pair of red shoes, and when we went to replace them, her foot was a half-size bigger. In the three and a half months since her transplant, our lives had once again settled into a deceptively normal routine. I wanted to believe it was going to last, but I smelled the not-knowing in the air. Dr. Kamalaker had scheduled a routine X-ray and CT scan for the following week.

Sitting in church, I stared at the huge cross that hung from the ceiling behind Laurajane. I had never appreciated more fully the Christian story of the Easter resurrection. If God was capable of raising Jesus from the dead, couldn't He save Hannah, too?

And if He could, what was He waiting for?

"Thy will be done," I prayed from the bottom of my heart, knowing even as I said it that what I was really trusting was that His will was also my own.

Say Yes

CLAUDE'S SNORES WERE COMING FROM HANNAH'S ROOM; the two of them had fallen asleep halfway through her bedtime story. Will was waiting for me to tuck him in, and I knew why.

Less than a week ago, a few days after Easter, Dr. Kamalaker had slid a piece of film under the clip of a light board and pointed to the spot where the cancer had metastasized. At the time of Hannah's transplant, Claude and I had made a commitment not to subject her to any more treatments, but that was then; we asked Dr. Kamalaker to schedule another surgery immediately.

Early this morning, Claude had loaded our suitcases, Hannah's and mine, into the minivan for the trip to the hospital. I had walked Will to his friend Jeff's house, given him a kiss, and reminded him that Lili would pick him up after school. But when school was over, Lili was not there; Claude, Hannah, and I were waiting instead.

Now, as Will tossed his pile of stuffed animals onto the other twin bed to make room for me, I could see he had been crying. Easing my pregnant body next to him, I gathered him into my arms.

"Oh, Muffin," I said, kissing the top of his head, savoring his little-boy softness.

"Mom," he said, his voice muffled against my chest, "why didn't the doctors do Hannah's surgery?"

Part of me was desperate to avoid this conversation, but I knew Will was trusting me to be honest with him, and he deserved to know.

"Well," I said, choosing my words carefully, "Hannah's lump is in a different place this time. It has grown very close to Hannah's spinal cord and is wrapped around some very important veins. The doctors can't take this one out."

"But, Mom," Will cried, lifting his head to look at me, "can't they at least take out part of it?" He paused. "If they don't," he said slowly and deliberately, "Hannah's going to die."

My eyes filled with tears. I took a breath and choked them back. I wanted to be with Will in his pain. I didn't want to overwhelm him with my own.

"The truth is, Will," I said, picking my way slowly through the darkness that was threatening to engulf me, "no matter what we do, the doctors think Hannah only has a few months to live. If we do surgery, even to take some of the lump out, it means Hannah will be in a lot more pain between now and when she dies than if we do nothing."

Will threw his arms around my neck and sobbed. I felt as if my heart might drown in his pain. Waves of anger surged through me. Wasn't it enough for God that Hannah was going to die? Did He have to take Will's six-year-old innocence, too?

From infancy, Will had seemed more mature than other kids his age, but now, I would have given anything for him to know much less than he did. Months before, when Hannah first got sick, I had given him a blank journal and encouraged him to draw his feelings in it. For a long time, he hadn't made any entries. Recently, though, he had begun to share some of his pictures with me. The earliest ones were mostly intricate sketches of wounded or bleeding baseball players or American Indians, but just before Easter he had drawn an elaborate cross alongside what looked like a war memorial with an American flag. Underneath, he had carefully printed Hannah's name.

"I am so sorry, Will," I said when I finally felt able to speak. "I wish I could have told you anything else, but I believe you deserve to know the truth. That way, you have the same chance that Dad and I have to appreciate Hannah while she's here."

"It's just not fair," Will cried, shaking his fists in the air. "Hannah wants to be a big sister so much. Is she going to live long enough to see our new baby?"

"I don't know, Will," I said, amazed by how much he had already thought through. "The only thing I know to do is pray that she does."

"I *have* been praying, Mom," Will cried, "but how can God expect us to believe in Him if He's going to let Hannah die? I'll hate Him if He does."

I nodded, admiring his courage for having said it out loud, but offering a prayer to God just in case. I was feeling less and less sure of my faith. I wasn't about to run the risk of pissing Him off.

"Mom, does Hannah *know* she's going to die?" Will asked, his sobs subsiding.

"I'm not sure, but I think she does," I told him.

"Well, I don't want anyone to tell her, because I don't want her to be scared."

"I can appreciate that, Will," I told him, "but I also believe that if Hannah doesn't already know, she's going to figure it out. If she asks me, I'll have to tell her the truth. I don't want her to know she's going to die and not be able to talk to someone about it."

Will thought for a moment. "Yeah, I guess that's okay," he finally agreed. "But Mom, when you know that Hannah knows, will you tell me? I want her to be able to talk to *me* about it, too."

"It's a deal," I said, hugging him.

He was quiet.

"Mom, if all of our grandmas and grandpas are still alive, who is Hannah going to know in heaven?"

"Hmm," I said, shaking my head, "that's a good question." I paused. "Well, your *great*-grandparents are in heaven, right?"

"Yes, but Hannah probably won't know them."

"I guess that's true," I said, thinking as fast as I could. "I wonder if Bub, our kitty that died, will be there?"

Will rested his chin in the palm of his hand and stared into space.

"Yes, I think Bub will be there," he said finally, "and I guess, if you believe the Bible, Jesus will be there, too." He sounded skeptical.

"Don't forget the babies you miscarried, Mom," he added, his eyes wide open with excitement at the thought. "Even though we never met them in person, they're our brothers and sisters, too. Wow, that's *cool*! Hannah's going to get to meet them before we do!"

He threw his arms around me.

"Thanks, Mom. I feel a lot better." He was quiet for a moment. I waited.

"Actually, Mom, I'm *glad* you told me," he said finally. "You know how Hannah always wants to sleep in my other bed and usually I say no? Well, from now on, I'm going to say yes whenever she asks."

Healing Service Hypocrite

CLAUDE, WILL, HANNAH, AND I FOLLOWED LAURAJANE DOWN the center aisle to the chairs that had been reserved in the front row. Hannah was wearing her new red-and-pink-flowered Easter dress, white tights, and her red patent leather Mary Janes. She held my hand while we walked, barely able to contain her excitement; she knew this service was for her. Will, looking handsome and serious in his freshly ironed shirt, blue jacket, tie, and crisply creased chinos, followed behind with Claude. His crew cut had grown out, and although his hair was still short, he had spent a lot of time in front of the bathroom mirror earlier, parting, wetting, and combing it.

As we reached our seats, I turned to look at the congregation. The sanctuary was filled, mostly with people we knew. The crowd had fallen silent when we entered, their hush respectful and curious. I was grateful for the attention. Hannah's cancer was now the center of my world; I appreciated that, at least in this moment, it seemed to be the center of everyone else's, too.

The news of Hannah's inoperable tumor had shaken our community. So many people had asked Laurajane what they could do to help that she thought of offering a healing service for Hannah at our church. When she first told Claude and me about it, I wasn't sure it was a good idea. Although I loved the idea of people gathering to support one another, I was afraid that calling it a "healing" service would create impossible expectations. To me, "healing" meant a cure; I didn't want anyone to consider Hannah, Laurajane, or themselves a failure if Hannah died.

I was worried about Laurajane, too, concerned that she was putting too much pressure on herself, perhaps even challenging God. I remembered our conversation in the intensive care unit, when she had wondered about how well she knew Him, whether she was up to the task of being a minister. I hated the thought of her or anyone else using Hannah as a test case for their faith.

I also believed that, no matter what we did, prayer was not going to save Hannah.

Still, sitting at the front of the church, I could feel a genuine sense of love and care coming from everyone in the room. I wished I didn't feel like such a hypocrite in their midst. Glancing over at Claude, his fists clenched, his eyes tightly closed, tears sliding down his cheeks, I worried that he might accuse me of poisoning the whole pot if he knew what I was thinking; I also worried that he would be right. For the first time in his life, Claude had been reading the Bible and praying every day. I knew he would let Satan suck the heart out of his chest if it would save Hannah's life. My faith felt hollow and small compared to his.

The organist started to play, and everyone stood to sing. Hannah tugged at the hem of my dress.

"Pick me up, Mom," she said. "I want to see who's here."

Lifting her onto my hip, I balanced the hymnal on my burgeoning belly. Will took the book from my hand and held it up for me to see. I smiled at him gratefully.

"Oh, Mommy, look," Hannah whispered loudly, peering and pointing over my shoulder, "there's Nurse Amy, Dr. Kamalaker, Dr. Edman, and Dr. Markoff . . . and Mrs. Fisher and Mrs. Forsythe, Jackie and Jeff and their mom and dad . . ."

She squirmed and twisted to get a better view. Laurajane began her message, but it was hard for me to hear. Hannah was still whispering the names of everyone she recognized in my ear. Finally, when Laurajane began to recite the Lord's Prayer, Hannah paused. Turning to face the cross, she clasped her hands, bowed her head, and in a loud, clear voice, recited the prayer word for word. Hearing her, I felt proud and oddly reassured. If Hannah was going to die, surely it would count for something that she knew the Lord's Prayer.

It was time for the children to sing. Hannah and Will joined the others on the carpeted steps at the front of the church for a rousing rendition of "Jesus Loves Me." Will stood proudly and protectively behind Hannah, resting his hands on her shoulders. I felt proud of the two of them, and grateful to see so many children at this service. It seemed a fitting tribute to the way that Hannah's illness hadn't been hushed up and tucked away as if being sick were something to be afraid or ashamed of.

Rick, one of the more conservative members of our congregation, stood and asked for a microphone. My smile froze on my face. Every cell in my body screamed "Warning, warning." Rick started speaking.

"God is capable of working a miracle, right here, right now."

This was exactly what I'd been afraid of. Our faith was being hijacked; it was all on the line. I breathed deeply into my rising panic, and let myself hear Rick's words.

". . . Love," he said, "is the source of all healing." I exhaled and felt my resistance begin to slip away.

He motioned for us to come up to the altar. Hannah bounced out of her seat. She was loving being the center of attention. Will followed close behind, Claude and I more slowly. Laurajane stood, placing her hands on top of Hannah's head. Hannah closed her eyes. Offering a prayer for Hannah's healing, Laurajane invited Claude, Will, and me to join her. When all four of us had placed our hands on Hannah's head, Rick motioned for everyone in the second row to come up. They gathered in a circle around Laurajane, Claude, Will, and me, placing their hands on our shoulders. Gradually everyone in the sanctuary rose and came to the front of the church, forming circles around circles.

While death is inevitable, knowing you are loved is not.

When I saw Hannah's radiant face in the center of that circle, I realized that healing can happen even without a cure. No matter when Hannah died, she would die knowing that her life had mattered, that she was completely loved. I couldn't imagine a more profound healing than that.

. . . And the Cow Jumped
over the Moon

A FEW DAYS LATER A PACKAGE ARRIVED, ADDRESSED TO
"Miss Hannah Martell." It was from someone in Colorado.
Curious. I didn't think we knew anyone in Colorado.
Hannah unwrapped and opened it.

"Oh, look, Mommy," she said, "it's the cow jumping
over the moon!"

She lifted a beautiful, child-size quilt into the air for me
to see. It was an exquisite piece of work. The fabric on one
side was cream with light pink flowers and moss-colored
ivy. The other side was a delightful patchwork of green,
orange, lavender, and pink, surrounded by a border with
green, purple, and blue cows leaping over crescent moons
and white stars in a pink sky. Someone had put a great deal
of time and effort into making it. I wondered who.

At the bottom of the box was a manila envelope con-
taining a handwritten note and a cassette tape. I scanned
the note and then ran to the garage where Claude was
changing the oil in his car.

"Read this," I said breathlessly, handing him the note

and the tape. He frowned and wiped his hands on a towel. I watched his eyes scan the note as mine had done and then return to the beginning, taking his time. Halfway through, he started to cry.

The note was from one of Claude's cousins, someone he hadn't seen in years. She told us that when she first heard that Hannah was sick, she had decided she would make a quilt for her. As the months passed, her life had become busier and her heart heavier; she had begun to think she would never get to finish the quilt before Hannah died. Then, a week ago last Sunday, she wrote, she had gone to church. As soon as the service was over, an elderly woman she recognized but didn't know had approached her.

"I know you don't know me," the woman said, handing Claude's cousin a package, "but for some reason I can't explain, I know I need to give this to you."

She continued, "I make quilts, and some time ago, I felt compelled to make this one. It's for a young child; that's all I know. The whole time I was making it, I was wondering whose it was. I *still* don't know, but as I sat in church last week, *something told me that you do.*"

Claude's cousin started to cry. She told the woman the story of Hannah and the quilt she was wanting to give her. Then the woman started to cry, too. The story was so extraordinary that Claude's cousin had gone home and recorded the details of it onto the tape she had included with the quilt in the box, "just in case, when you tell the story, people don't believe you."

Holding the tape in my hand, I realized I didn't have to

prove anything to myself or anyone else. Suddenly I understood the reading I had heard so often in church: "Faith is the substance of things hoped for, the evidence of things not seen." The quilt's presence at the foot of Hannah's bed was enough evidence for me.

Mother's Day

HANNAH WAS STANDING NEXT TO THE OAK TABLE IN OUR
front hall, holding a plate of Noah's Ark cookies. Someone
had left a box of them, still warm from the oven, on our
porch the day before. They were sugar cookies, perfect for
us to bring to the preschool Mother's Day Tea. I was holding a camcorder, capturing the moment on video. The
camera, like my journal, had been documenting the past
year of Hannah's life in fits and starts. Hannah's diagnosis
and subsequent relapses had prompted flurries of photo ops
and journal entries that were then followed by long,
dormant periods when, lulled by the apathy of routine, I
would begin to feel that there would always be more time.
I knew differently now.

Hannah set the plate on the table and wiped her hands
on the front of her dress.

"How do I look, Mommy?" she asked.

"You look beautiful, Missy," I said.

Her cheeks were rosy, her eyes bright. She had been
spending so much time outside that the May sun had

already tanned her skin. These days, people who didn't know us were complimenting Hannah on her "haircut." It was still very short, but it had grown in enough to lie flat on her head, like Tinkerbell's in Disney's *Peter Pan*. Her dress, printed with tiny purple violets, had an Empire waist, a large lace collar, and a matching headband. She smiled at the camera and patted the bow of the headband.

"See my hair and my hair bow," she said, "and my dress," she continued, smoothing the front of it, "and my tights and my red shoes," she said, holding one leg out, like a ballerina, for the camera to see. She let her arms hang at her sides for a moment and stared silently into the camera. Then she reached for the cookies.

"Come on, Mommy, we can't be late for the tea."

I turned off the camera and kneeled down to arrange it properly in its case. Hannah came over and stood next to me, draping her arm around my neck.

"You look beautiful, too, Mommy," she said.

"Thank you, Missy," I said, giving her a hug.

Earlier that morning, as I stood in my closet wondering what to wear, I had realized that this might be one of the last things I would do publicly as Hannah's mother. I thought of all the ceremonies and graduations that I would never attend, when Hannah's name would never be called. I decided to make the most of this opportunity. While Hannah sat on the edge of my bed, I slipped the most beautiful maternity dress I owned over my head. It was made of ivory and peach silk. I carefully applied my makeup, dotted my wrists with perfume, and placed a light pink hat with a wide, floppy brim on my head. Hannah clapped her hands together and gasped.

"Mommy, that's perfect," she whispered.

I heard Claude coming up the steps, two at a time, already late for work. He peeked in the door.

"Just wanted to give my girls a kiss before I leave," he said. Then, noticing our finery, he smiled and let out a whistle.

Hannah squealed and jumped to the floor.

"Before you go, check how tall I am today, Daddy," she said, standing as straight as she could, lifting her chin toward the ceiling.

Claude laughed and stood behind her, drawing the flat of his hand across the top of her head to a spot just above the buckle of his belt.

"Whoa, Missy," he exclaimed, as she turned to see. "You're taller than my belt buckle today."

Hannah giggled and danced in front of him. It didn't seem to matter to either of them that they had repeated the same routine every day for weeks. It was almost as if Hannah sensed Claude's fierce resistance to thinking about her death. Their time together was about being silly and having fun.

Hannah was giggling now as Claude scooped her up.

"I love you, Missy," he said softly.

"I love you, too, Daddy," she said.

Holding Hannah's hand as we walked to school, I felt so blessed to be her mom. How would I ever be able to let her go? In spite of my initial skepticism at the healing service and the certainty in my heart that Hannah was going to die, I couldn't help hoping for a miracle. Hope, I realized now, was the irrepressible substance of faith. It welled up naturally in response to fear and uncertainty, returning again and again, like a living thing.

Waiting to Exhale

HANNAH WAS SKIPPING IN CIRCLES AROUND THE KITCHEN while I prepared dinner. The window above the sink was open to the early June breeze. The clanging lid on the soup pot and the steaming smells suggested all was well.

I was beginning to think the doctors were wrong. Hannah didn't look sick. She hadn't so much as sneezed in weeks. Her hair, which last month had lain flat on her head, had grown at least an inch longer and now had a personality of its own; Claude called it "woolly mammoth" hair because it stuck up and out all over. She was eating well, gaining weight, and getting taller; the hem of her "robe j's" swung freely at her ankles now. She had even participated in her preschool Olympics a few days earlier, the only competitor to run in red patent leather shoes.

For the first time in months, I had regained a sense of privacy in my life. Although I felt grateful for everyone's help while Hannah was sick, I had sometimes felt as if my whole life was being lived in a storefront window. Friends and family had cleaned my house, rearranged my cupboards, and washed my dirty underwear. During Hannah's bone marrow transplant, not wanting to leave her alone, Claude and I had made love standing up in the tiny bathroom connected to Hannah's hospital room.

One of the ways I had found to maintain a sense of myself was to withhold the extent of my pain from others. It had been one of my guiltiest pleasures to tell people that I was "fine" even when I wasn't. Although I knew it wasn't the truth, it kept me from feeling like a gigantic wound that wouldn't stop hemorrhaging. It was much easier to say, and people looked so relieved when I did. Lately, I had been saying the same thing, except that now I was beginning to believe it.

I stirred the soup. Suddenly Hannah stopped skipping and doubled over. She coughed once, twice, three times, then stood up and cleared her throat. I rested the spoon on the edge of the stove, my brow creased with suspicion. A car honked. A dog barked. Hannah's sequined tutu sparkled in the late afternoon sun. Lifting a clenched fist to her mouth, she cleared her throat once more.

"It's okay, Mommy," she said finally. "I just have a cough that won't come out."

Her red shoes clicked across the linoleum. I bent down and gathered her up. She felt solid and strong in my arms. I inhaled her sweetness, cherry lollipops and baby shampoo, and lost myself in her embrace. The soup? It boiled over.

Grandma's Promise

MY MOTHER AND HANNAH WERE SITTING ON THE FLOOR OF
Hannah's room. The Barbie doll box was tipped upside
down, spilling dolls, clothes, and tiny pastel shoes across the
rug. The two of them were dressing the Barbies for an out-
ing to the Barbie mall that Hannah had arranged in a corner by the door. Hannah was still wearing her bathing suit.
We had spent the afternoon at the pool, watching Will,
Grandpa, and Uncle Ben cannonball and belly-flop off the
diving boards.

Ever since Will was a year old, he had spent the first week
of July at the Cherry Festival in Traverse City, Michigan,
with my parents. He had begged to be allowed to go again
this year. I had no doubt that it would be good for him.
Claude and I were doing our best to give him love and
attention, but we couldn't deny the fact that our focus was
mostly on Hannah. Her health seemed to be degenerating
slowly but steadily. Each day she tired more quickly and
coughed more frequently. I was tired, too. My body was
full and heavy with the baby that was due any day. While

Hannah and I were content to sleep and snuggle, Will was understandably restless.

I had struggled with the decision. I didn't want Will to miss the birth of our baby, and I definitely wanted him to be with us for Hannah's death. Since the doctors couldn't tell us exactly when either of these things was going to happen, I had to trust my intuition. Claude and I took a leap of faith and enlisted both sets of grandparents to help. My parents and brother Ben had agreed to drive from Michigan to New Jersey to pick Will up, and Claude's parents had agreed to bring him back ten days later.

Hannah set her doll on the floor in front of her and looked at my mother.

"Will you promise me something, Grandma?" Hannah asked.

"Sure, Hannah," my mother said, focusing on the half-dressed Barbie on her knee.

"No, Grandma. I want you to *promise* me something," Hannah said quietly.

My mother looked up. Hannah's eyes were on her, intent, serious.

"Yes, Hannah," she said. "Anything."

Hannah was silent. My mother waited.

"Grandma," Hannah said finally, "I want you to promise that you'll never forget me."

My mother's eyes filled with tears. Hannah's were dry, resting on her grandmother, waiting for her reply.

"I promise, Hannah. I will never forget," my mother finally said.

Circle of Life

I AWOKE JUST BEFORE DAWN WITH LABOR PAINS, KNOWING that today was the day. I called Nurse Katie, who had offered to stay with Hannah while Claude and I went to the hospital. There was no point in calling Will. He and his grandparents were already on the road, headed back to us. They were not scheduled to arrive in New Jersey until the following day.

The streets were quiet in the first light. While Claude loaded the car, I wrote out the instructions for Hannah's medication. Four days earlier, Dr. Kamalaker had started her on Tylenol with codeine, but despite the fact that she was taking it every four hours, Hannah could barely walk, she was in so much pain. Yesterday, we had called Pat, Hannah's hospice nurse. She was scheduled to come to our house this evening to instruct us on how to give Hannah morphine. I now had my fingers crossed that this baby would be born quickly, and we would be home by then.

Hannah woke just as Katie arrived. I gave her a kiss as she crawled onto Katie's lap.

"Call me as soon as the baby comes," Hannah said.

After five breathtaking hours of labor, Margaret Rose slid, wet and wailing, into the world. She was beautiful, almost eight pounds, with lots of hair, sturdy legs, chubby cheeks, and perfect rosebud lips. Claude wiped his eyes with the back of his sleeve and couldn't stop smiling. As I held my littlest girl, her slippery skin against mine, for one long, perfect moment I wanted nothing more.

While the nurses wiped and wrapped Margaret, Claude called Hannah.

"Congratulations, Hannah. You're a big sister now," Claude said. "Our baby's name is Margaret Rose."

"Oh, goody," Hannah said. "A girl, just like Briar Rose. Okay, tell Margaret that me and Nurse Katie will be there right away."

"No, Hannah," Claude interrupted, "you don't need to come. The doctors have said that Mom and Margaret are well enough to come home today. You and Katie can wait there. We'll be home as soon as we can."

An hour later, standing in the hospital nursery watching the nurses bathe and weigh Margaret, Claude heard someone banging wildly on the window. He looked up to see Hannah in Katie's arms, grinning and waving, wearing a huge button that read "I'm a Big Sister."

"I tried to tell her she didn't have to come, but she insisted," Katie said. "Hannah told me that, because she and Will had gone to the 'Big Brother/Big Sister' class, she *knew* that one of the most important jobs a big sister has is to visit the new baby at the hospital."

"What about her pain?" Claude asked.

"She told me 'bring the pills just in case,' " Katie said.

"Oh, one more thing," Katie said. "You didn't mention it, so I don't know if you knew, but Will and his grandparents called. They left Michigan a day sooner than they had originally planned. They'll be at your house this afternoon."

While I waited for our release to be processed, Claude headed home to meet Will and his parents. Hannah asked to stay. She took a dose of pain medication and fell asleep on the bed with Margaret and me.

Holding my girls, I couldn't believe how lucky I was. I knew there were so many other ways things might have happened, and I hadn't been alone in my worry. When I had first shared the news of our pregnancy, some people's eyes glazed over. There is no polite way to say, "You're crazy. What were you thinking?"

When the doctors gave Hannah only three months to live, it hadn't taken me more than a second to calculate that this baby was going to be born just when Hannah was expected to die. It had seemed an impossible situation. Yet, the decision Claude and I had made to get pregnant hadn't been made in our minds; it had been made in our hearts. I could only trust that the God who had a hand in all of it would be there to see us through, one way or another.

Now, listening to the breath of my little girl on one side and my baby girl on the other, I knew that only the most awesome grace could have arranged this day: both my girls in the same world, and Will coming home.

Metamorphosis

I WAS SITTING IN A ROCKING CHAIR IN OUR BEDROOM, nursing Margaret, who was a week old. Will was sitting on the floor, staring out the window. A picture book about dinosaurs lay open at his feet. Hannah was on the bed, lying in a half-seated position against a pile of pillows, covered by her pink blanket. Her eyes were closed, but I didn't think she was asleep.

Several days before, she had announced, "I hurt too much. I want to sleep in the bed that smells like you and Daddy."

Her tumor was growing rapidly now, large enough to press against her ribs and spinal cord. Although a constant dose of morphine was being pumped into her body, twenty-four hours a day, Hannah could no longer walk; she had to be carried. Other than asking to go to the toilet, she seemed content to stay where she was.

I felt frustrated that there wasn't more I could do to help Hannah, and longed for information about how to prepare her and us for her death. Pat had given me what she could, but the hospice she worked for rarely dealt with dying children; none of the hospices in our area did. It seemed almost inconceivable to me that there had been shelves of books, videos, and even classes at the hospital to prepare Hannah for Margaret's birth. Where were the experts now, when I needed to prepare her for her death?

I had done my best to anticipate what Hannah might need. The antique rocking chair was a testament to that. It had always been Hannah's favorite spot to snuggle and read. I had asked Claude to bring it upstairs, imagining it would be the perfect place for us to spend her final days. I was wrong. "It hurts too much," she said. My image of us rocking peacefully into her death was simply one more thing I had to let go of.

Will looked up.

"Mom, how long does it take a body to become a skeleton?"

Hannah heard Will's question. Her eyes popped open. These days, death was one of her favorite subjects.

You've got to be kidding, I thought. I was all for telling the truth and facing fears; but I wasn't ready for *this* conversation.

"I'm not sure, Will," I said, feeling that I didn't want to know, either.

He screwed up his lips and creased his brow, as if he were contemplating probable rates of decomposition. Hannah had her own ideas.

"You know," she said, her eyes bright with mischief, "they can bury your body, but they can't bury your spirit!"

She was grinning. Will looked at her and grinned, too.

"That's great, Hannah," he said. He turned to me.

"What do you think, Mom? Do our spirits go to heaven even though our bodies are buried?"

I had been waiting for this question for a while. I had even wondered if I should bring it up myself. I loved that the two of them had done it on their own.

"Well," I began, my thoughts tripping seven sentences ahead of my words, "I believe that when the body is too sick or too old to live anymore, it dies, and then the soul is free."

"What happens to the soul after the body dies, Mom?" Will asked.

"I'm not really sure," I admitted. "Some people believe that souls go to heaven after the body dies. I think I believe that, too."

"Me, too," said Hannah.

Will wanted to know more. "I know the Bible says that, but does anybody else?" he asked.

"Well," I answered, "I've been reading books about something called a 'near-death experience.' Sometimes people die for a few minutes, like in very serious surgeries or car accidents, but then doctors manage to bring them back to life. When this happens, those people describe death as a long tunnel with a bright light at the other end that draws them into a place of beautiful love. Not everyone believes that's what happens. I guess we can't be sure until we do it ourselves."

I continued. "You know how a butterfly grows inside

the cocoon until it's ready to fly? Or the way a hermit crab lives in a shell until it gets too small for his growing body and then moves to another? I like to think death is something like that."

"I'm going to be a butterfly," Hannah stated, and with that settled, rolled back onto the pillows and shut her eyes.

On the Threshold

HANNAH WAS DOZING ON ONE SIDE OF THE BED, HER LONG legs barely covered by her pink blanket. She was wearing only a pair of cotton underpants.

"Clothes are too scratchy," she had said.

One of her arms lay across Margaret, who was asleep next to her, tightly bundled in fuzzy pink pajamas. The hum of the air conditioner in the window accounted for the nip in the air despite the fact that the late July sun was baking the roof overhead. The sicker Hannah got, the colder she wanted the room to be.

I rocked to the rhythm of the morphine pump's click. As Hannah's tumor grew, so did the amount of morphine she required. I was grateful for the way the drug seemed to dull Hannah's pain, but the more effective it was, the easier it was to deny that she was sick enough to die. For days now, I had fantasized that she might wake up, ask to get dressed, and suggest we all go out to dinner. Claude seemed even more lost in the fantasy. Every time Dr. Kamalaker had prescribed an increase in her dose, he questioned the need to do it, explaining that he was afraid she might get addicted. Nobody had the heart to tell him that addiction is not possible for someone who is dead.

I continued to rock back and forth. A stack of books on the dresser with titles like *Living With Death and Dying, Embraced by the Light,* and *How to Go on Living When Someone You Love Dies* was as neglected as the shriveled piece of cheese that Hannah had requested and then refused to eat. Even her Christmas dress, which she had asked me to hang on the curtain rod where she could see it, seemed to be holding its breath.

I closed my eyes. My lids felt heavy and warm from too little sleep. I could feel Hannah looking at me. I opened my eyes slowly. Her arms were outstretched, reaching for me.

"Mommy, I want you to carry me to my room."

I came alive. It was the first time in days she had asked to go anywhere other than the bathroom. Perhaps this was the moment everything had been waiting for. Hannah was taking an interest in life again. I gently and gingerly ran my hands under her bony hips and back and lifted her from the bed. I moved slowly to give her body time to adjust. I could almost hear her internal organs groan as the tumor shifted its bulk inside her. Hannah wrapped her thin arms around my neck and locked her legs around my hips. She pinned herself against me with a strength that surprised me. Her head rested on my shoulder. I breathed her in, felt her soft, "woolly mammoth" hair against my cheek. Her body was unnaturally warm given the coolness of the room. She was burning with a fever that would not break. Her chest rose and fell against mine, and I could feel both of our hearts beating—mine slow and deep, hers quick and light.

As I lifted her from the bed, I tried to imagine her sitting on the floor of her room, surrounded by baby dolls and dress-up clothes. I knew the image was as fragile as a painter's wet canvas. As I adjusted Hannah's position on my hip, she winced. The image slid out of my mind. I tried desperately not to jiggle or jar her too much as I carried her down the stairs. When we got to the doorway of her room, Hannah reached out and grabbed the wooden molding.

"Don't put me down and don't go in," she said. "I just want to look."

The two of us stood on the threshold, watching dust dance in the late afternoon sun. A pink comforter and her cow-jumping-over-the-moon quilt stretched neatly, without wrinkles, across her bed. Dolls and stuffed animals stared blankly from their perches on the shelf. Two seashells from a preschool field trip leaned against each other on top of her dresser. The magic wand she had made at her birthday party almost a year ago lay in the middle of the floor. I wanted to wave it through the hush and bring everything back to life.

I knew she was saying good-bye, but I wasn't ready. This room with its sugar-pink sweetness, Barbie dolls, and red patent leather shoes *was* Hannah. If I were to say good-bye to this, what part of her would be left?

Releasing her grip on the door frame, Hannah wrapped her arms around my neck, and buried her face in my shoulder.

"I'm ready to go back now," she said.

As we climbed the stairs, I walked as slowly as I could, savoring the closeness of her. Before returning her to the nest of pillows and blankets, I stood silently, swaying from side to side, as if in a trance. I didn't want to let her go. I wanted to remain in this moment forever.

I thought about her room, how possible and yet inconceivable it was that she would never see it again. I wondered if it would always wait for her to return, if it would always be her room, if it would ever forget. I wondered the same things about myself: if I could accept that she would never return, if I would always feel like her mother, if I would ever forget.

Everywhere I Am,
There You'll Be

❧

I WAS SITTING AT THE FOOT OF THE BED, SNUGGLING
Margaret. It was early in the day. Claude had left for work.
Will was sitting on the floor, eating cereal and watch-
ing TV.

Hannah stirred and sat up slowly. I turned to look at her.
Her skin was almost translucent. She hadn't eaten more
than a bite or two of solid food for almost a week. As she
had grown thinner, her tumor had grown bigger. Her left
side was swollen grotesquely out of proportion. The skin
that stretched across her ribs was deep purple from the
mass of blood vessels that had accumulated there in a vain
attempt to sate the cancer's appetite for blood. Sometimes
she asked me to rub her side. I hated knowing that as I lov-
ingly ran my cool palms over her hot, numb skin, I was
gently caressing her tumor. Hannah had made friends with
it somehow, treating it gingerly, deferentially, adjusting her
pillows so it could rest on a cushion of softness. I wasn't
willing. I wanted it to be gone.

Hannah looked at me. She winced, and then smiled.

"Mommy," she said quietly, "do you know that even if I go to heaven, I'm going to come back?"

I paused before answering. I wanted to tell her the truth. The problem was, I wasn't sure exactly what the truth was. I had read that grieving children under the age of six imagine death as a short absence and expect loved ones to return sometime after the funeral. I wondered if this was what Hannah thought, too.

I took a breath. Hannah was grinning now, her head cocked to one side. I studied her face. She looked light, expectant, unconcerned. I felt as if she was reading my mind, and was amused by my dilemma. I closed my eyes for a moment. There, behind my eyelids, I saw something I could hardly believe: It was Hannah, dancing in the sparkly darkness, radiant, laughing, and waving. I grinned, my eyes still closed.

In that instant I knew that, no matter what happened, there was a part of Hannah that would always be with me, something of her that would never die. It wasn't a belief. It wasn't a hope. It was a knowing beyond the workings of my mind, the quietest, deepest experience of faith I had ever known.

I opened my eyes and let go of the breath I had been holding in my heart.

"Yes, Hannah, I know," I said.

Hannah leaned back into the pillows, closed her eyes, and smiled.

FAITH IS NOT ABOUT BELIEVING but about letting go of beliefs. Faith does not hope and pray for things to be different sometime in the future. Faith is the still heart that refuses nothing, our willingness to trust things as they are.

Compassion

from specialness to belonging

. . . It is assenting
that makes them angels . . .
their only work
to shine back,
however the passing brightness
hurts their eyes.

—Jane Hirshfield

As Real as It Gets

HANNAH WAS SPEAKING LESS AND LESS; EVERY WORD FROM her now might be her last.

"Mommy, where's Will?" she asked, her voice almost a whisper.

Will rolled over and sat up. He had been lying on the floor, watching a movie, the volume so low it was practically mute.

"I'm right here, Hannah," he said softly, turning off the TV.

Hannah shifted her head to the side, just enough to face him. They looked at each other quietly.

"Will," Hannah asked, "do you know I'm too sick to ever play again?"

I was afraid to speak, afraid to breathe, wondering what Will would say.

"Yes, Hannah, I know," he said quietly. "Does that make you sad?"

Hannah paused, still looking at him.

"No," she said, shaking her head.

The two of them turned to me. I could feel their eyes taking in the wisps of hair that had escaped the clasp of my barrette, my creased forehead, heavy eyelids, and pale skin. I didn't feel as tired as I knew I looked. I felt awed; humbled by the simplicity with which they had stepped into one of the most intimate moments two people could share. In one breath, the two of them had shown me what telling the truth and living the truth were ultimately all about.

Sorry She Asked

I KNOW SHE MEANT WELL; SHE SIMPLY HAD NO WAY OF knowing.

When the well-dressed, middle-aged woman stepped into the elevator with us at JCPenney that Sunday afternoon, things were not what they seemed. She smiled sweetly at me and peeked at baby Margaret in my arms.

She winked and turned to Will, who was eyeing her curiously.

"You must be the big brother," she said with exaggerated importance. "Your mother is so lucky to have two beautiful children."

"I have another sister at home," Will said proudly. "Her name is Hannah."

"Ooohhh," said the nice lady, "why isn't she shopping, too?"

I could see it coming and needed a Miss Manners book fast. Will didn't hesitate. He jumped right in.

"She's at home with my dad. She's dying." He added

helpfully, "We're here to get an outfit for my baby sister Margaret to wear to Hannah's funeral."

The woman turned to me, the skin on her face two shades lighter than her makeup. I felt sorry for her and smiled as sympathetically as I could. She wasn't ready to let it go. She arched her brows and pasted a cheery smile on her face.

"Well," she said loudly, "I bet you're grateful for the babies you've had."

There was no stopping Will now. "That's for sure," he said emphatically. "My mom's had four miscarriages, too!"

Looking as if she might be sick, the woman turned and punched the second-floor button. When the doors slid open, she brushed past a group of people waiting to get in and disappeared down the hall.

"She was a nice lady, wasn't she, Mom?" Will said, taking my hand.

"Yes, she was," I said, "but I wonder if it was hard for her to hear about my miscarriages and Hannah dying."

"Maybe," Will said, shrugging his shoulders. "But she was the one who asked."

The Bathroom Guilt Trip

I HAD TO GO TO THE BATHROOM, BUT I WAS AFRAID TO leave. It was clear to everyone that Hannah was dying, but no one could tell me when.

A small light was still burning in the corner of the bedroom for Pat, the hospice nurse, who had already come and gone. Every night, she checked in at two a.m. I was always awake when she came. We would whisper quietly so we wouldn't wake Claude or the kids. All of us were sleeping in the same room now: Will and Claude in sleeping bags on the floor and Margaret, Hannah, and I in the bed.

Earlier tonight, I had asked Pat the question I always asked: "How much longer?" She had given me the answer she always gave: "It could happen anytime."

I chided myself now for not having gone to the bathroom then. I had heard about children who lingered near death for days and chose to die in the one moment they were left alone. If I were to go to the bathroom now and Hannah died while I was gone, could I live with having to tell people that, instead of dying peacefully in my arms,

Hannah died while I was on the toilet? I decided to hold it a while longer.

I watched Hannah breathe, imagining every breath to be her last. I saw how she looked already dead in the long, irregular pauses between breaths: thin, translucent, not breathing. I reminded myself that if she were dead, she would feel no pain. I began to tell myself that Hannah's death might not be such a bad thing; that it would be okay with me if she were to remain in her breathless, painless translucence.

I was feeling more desperate to go to the bathroom and guilty for having imagined Hannah dead. How could my body even *think* about relieving itself when Hannah's body was struggling to breathe? I lay next to her, praying for her breath to stop, then praying it would continue. I felt as if God were waiting for me to make up my mind; I couldn't decide which would be better.

Now I *really* had to go. Every minute I told myself, "If you had gone two minutes ago, you could have done it, and she would still be here."

When I couldn't wait another second, I ran to the bathroom and sat on the toilet, barely able to contain the extent of my guilt and my relief.

Then I returned to Hannah's side. She was still breathing. I felt a rush of gratitude followed by a crushing pain. How could I have wished even one more moment of this distorted life on her? I began to sob, overwhelmed by grief, guilt, and frustration. I buried my face in a pillow, not wanting to wake anyone. Hannah moaned. I sobbed harder. I had never felt more frightened or alone.

Suddenly, a feeling of warmth flooded through me. I lifted my face from the pillow, certain that this unexpected peace must be a sign that Hannah had died. I was wrong. She was still breathing. I closed my eyes. The warmth remained. I knew then that I wasn't alone; that whatever was going to happen, it wasn't up to me. The only thing I could do was be with Hannah; everything else was in God's hands.

Stillness

I LIFTED HANNAH OFF THE TOILET, GENTLY, SPREADING MY hands wide under her hips so that her weight would be distributed more evenly. She winced.

"I'm sorry, Hannah," I said. She nodded but didn't speak.

Throughout her illness, even during her bone marrow transplant, Hannah had refused to wear a diaper.

"Diapers are for babies," she had said.

Days ago, Pat had suggested to me that perhaps it was finally time. Hannah hadn't even waited for me to respond.

"No diapers," she said.

"What about a catheter?" Pat asked.

Hannah leaned toward Pat, looking directly into her eyes.

"No diapers and no tubes. *Ever*. You have to promise," she said.

Now, as I stood up, I could feel Hannah's heart racing against my chest. Before I could maneuver her long legs through the doorway, Hannah leaned over my shoulder and looked in the mirror. She urged me to move closer. I obeyed.

Hannah hadn't seen herself in weeks. As the two of us stared silently at her reflection, she seemed surprised, not frightened, by what she saw. She tipped her head to one side, slightly puzzled, even amused. I couldn't take my eyes off her; it was as if I, too, were seeing her for the first time. Her blond hair was dull and dry, sticking up all over her head. Her skin was pale, almost blue, the right side of her face gaunt, skin stretched taut over bone, the left side collapsed.

As our eyes met in the mirror, she looked into me the way she had when she blew out the candles on her cake almost eleven months before. I knew then that Hannah was more than this frail, sick child I was holding; part of her was living beyond this suffering, in that stillness I could feel but could not see.

Silence

THE HOUSE WAS QUIET AND SMELLED LIKE ICE RIPENING. I wrote in my journal and watched Hannah breathe. Although it had been less than three weeks since Claude carried her upstairs, it felt as if she had been dying forever. I glanced at the clock. Two o'clock. Will was playing at a friend's house and Margaret was asleep in one corner of the bed. Exhausted from too many sleepless nights, I closed my eyes and rocked, resting my head on the back of the chair.

Suddenly, Hannah moaned. My eyes flew open. Hannah was reaching for me. I jumped up, checking the morphine pump and Broviac tubes to make sure nothing had malfunctioned.

"Does it hurt, baby?" I asked, stroking the top of her head. "Should I push the button and give you more morphine?"

Hannah nodded, still moaning and reaching for me. I pushed the button. I was starting to feel scared. Although her condition had seemed stable when Dr. Kamalaker stopped by yesterday, something had drastically changed. I decided to pick her up, not knowing what else to do. I lifted her off the bed and sat on the edge of the mattress, resting her body on my lap. Placing a soft pillow between her head and my arm, I covered the rest of her with her pink blanket. Hannah stopped moaning. Although her breath sounded strange, rapid and shallow, her eyes were open, looking at me. I reached for the phone and called Claude at work.

"I think you should come home right away," I said.

Claude sighed. He sounded exasperated. This wasn't the first time I had made such a call. I felt a bit like a pregnant woman with too many false-alarm labors.

"Okay, as soon as I clear off my desk I'll be there," he said.

I made two more calls: one to Pat, the other to my friend Kate. Kate had been a godsend in the past year. She had done practically everything: delivered hot, home-cooked meals, watched my kids, arranged for a house-keeper, washed and folded our laundry, and mowed our lawn. Minutes after I hung up the phone, I heard her running up the stairs. When she opened the door and saw Hannah on my lap, Kate began to cry.

"Is this it?" she whispered.

"I don't know," I said. Kate picked up Margaret.

"We'll wait downstairs," she said.

"Could you do one other thing?" I asked. Kate nodded. "Will is at Lili's house, playing with Philippe. Please call, ask her to bring him home, and when he gets here, send him up right away."

Kate left the room, closing the door behind her. Hannah's eyes were open, watching me. Her breathing was more labored and irregular. I started to cry, and then, feeling helpless, I began to pray and sing. Hymns that I hadn't thought of since childhood, the Lord's Prayer, and the Twenty-third Psalm poured out of me.

The door opened, and Pat came in. Our eyes met, but neither of us said anything. She kneeled on the floor in front of me and gently examined Hannah, whose body was now thrashing intermittently. When she looked up, she had tears in her eyes, and I knew. Paging Dr. Kamalaker, she quietly explained what was happening, listened for a moment, nodding, and then hung up. There was a tentative knock on the door. Will stepped into the room. He looked at Hannah on my lap, and then at me.

"Is it time, Mom?" he asked.

"Yes, Will," I said.

Will bent down, stroked Hannah's hair, and kissed the top of her head.

"I love you, Hannah," he said. Her eyes rolled toward him. The two of them looked at each other for a moment, and then Will looked at me.

"Mom, I want to wait downstairs, but as soon as Hannah dies, come and get me, okay?"

I nodded. He kissed Hannah once more.

"Remember, Hannah, I love you," he said, then turned and left the room.

At ten minutes to three, Claude's car pulled into the

driveway. The door slammed. I heard his footsteps thud-
ding on the stairs. He threw open the door.

"What's happening?" he asked Pat, who was sitting on
the floor with the morphine pump.

"Hannah's dying," I said, more calmly than I could
believe. "She's been waiting for you. You have to tell her
it's okay to go."

Claude fell to his knees and let out a low moan. His
body shook with sobs. He lifted his head, leaned over, and
kissed her.

"It's time for you to go, Missy," he said. "Don't worry
about us. We love you. We're going to be okay."

Although Hannah's body continued to fight for twenty
more minutes, some part of her already felt free. Then, one
moment she was alive and breathing; the next, she wasn't.
I couldn't believe how unexpected it felt. I looked into
her eyes. Nothing but blue. The room had filled with an
almost palpable stillness that enveloped us in its thick, white
peace.

P.S.

I TURNED JUST AS WILL CAME IN. HE GLANCED AT HANNAH'S body on the bed, and then lifted his face toward the ceiling.

"Hi, Hannah," he said. "I know you're here. I'm glad you're not hurting anymore."

He sat on the edge of the bed next to Hannah's body.

"Is it okay for me to touch it, Mom?" he asked.

"Sure," I said.

I watched as he ran his fingers slowly over her arm, then stroked her hair and hands.

"When will she start to feel dead?" he asked.

"I don't know," I said, "but probably soon."

He stood and looked toward the ceiling again.

"Hey, Hannah, I'm going to have some pizza," he said. "I'll be back to check on you in a little while. We'll see if you're more dead then."

Amen

A SMALL GATHERING OF FRIENDS AND FAMILY WERE ASSEMbled at Hannah's grave on the morning of her burial. The sun was shining brightly, promising another hot day. Will and his cousins were jostling each other and giggling while they waited for the service to end. They were the same children who, the day before, had stood around Hannah's open casket at the funeral home. Encouraged by Will, some of them had stroked and poked Hannah's body. A few adults had looked on disapprovingly; they were the same ones who, now, were trying to shush the graveside commotion.

Claude and I had decided to bury Hannah rather than have her cremated. I wanted to be able to come to her grave and know that the little hands I had held and the form I had loved were there, even if they were underground. Claude, Will, and I had visited a couple of cemeteries before agreeing that we all preferred the smaller, quieter one. There had been some discussion about which plot to choose. Claude had liked the one nestled in a stand of pines. We had eventually agreed on the one Will preferred. It was situated between a small pond and a beautiful gazebo. "That way my kids will have somewhere to play when I come to visit Hannah," Will had explained.

Now, I nestled Margaret against my chest and glanced at Laurajane, whose head was bent in prayer. She looked very official in a long white robe, although, in the humidity, her hair was as wiry and unmanageable as ever. Standing at the edge of the hole where Hannah's body was about to be buried, I was trying to hold myself together. Before coming to the cemetery, Claude, Will, Margaret, and I had gone to the funeral home to see Hannah for the last time. I had decided to bury her in her Christmas dress with a pair of her red shoes, but I chose to keep her pink blanket. I was sure that she would understand; Will was now sleeping with it. Will had asked to close the casket. Before lowering the lid, he had placed one of his pillows under her head and laid a beaded Easter cross in her hand.

"Good-bye, Hannah. We'll miss you," he had said.

Out of the corner of my eye, I noticed that Wanda, the cemetery manager, had stood up. One of the things Claude had been emphatic about when we met with her was that, when it came to burying Hannah's body, he didn't want any mix-ups. He wanted to know for sure, when we drove away, that Hannah's body would remain in the grave we had left her in. Wanda had thought about it for a minute and then suggested that, short of burying Hannah ourselves, the best way to address Claude's concern would be for us to witness the closing of the concrete vault after Hannah's casket had been lowered into it. Claude and I had agreed.

What I'm certain Wanda told us, but I hadn't fully understood, was that this procedure involved a backhoe.

"Amen," Laurajane said. Wanda cleared her throat and stepped forward.

"Claude and Maria have asked to witness the closing of the vault," she said. "We're going to need some room, so if all of you would be kind enough to step back about ten feet . . ."

The rest of her words were drowned out by the cough and sputter of an unusually loud engine. From a spot in the distance behind a clump of trees, a backhoe, with a gigantic cement lid swinging from a chain affixed to its shovel, began chugging toward us. As the children started shriek-ing and running in circles, the adults stumbled over them-selves to get out of the way.

The backhoe continued its crawl toward us. While two cemetery employees lowered Hannah's casket into the concrete vault in the ground, the adults, now watching from a distance halfway up the hill, didn't know whether to look respectfully interested or politely away. The chil-dren, however, had moved in as close as they could. They high-fived each other, clapped, and cheered as the back-hoe operator expertly dropped the lid in the right spot on his first try.

Claude and I grinned at each other as I caught Laurajane's eye. Hannah had never hesitated to rewrite the rules; it seemed perfect that her burial had been no exception. I was sure that she would have giggled, too, at the backhoe touch at the end.

Vacuum

MARGARET AND I WERE LYING TOGETHER ON THE COUCH.
The Indian summer sun warmed the picture window glass
and spilled onto my lap. Exhausted, I dozed while Margaret
nursed. When she finished, I slipped my finger between
her lips, releasing the suction of her mouth on my breast.
A warm trickle of milk ran across her cheek. She stirred
and nuzzled me. Inhaling her sweetness, I began to cry. I
felt overwhelmed with love for this tiny baby who had so
effortlessly emerged in our lives and my heart. I felt a deep
sadness that these days with her were being swallowed by
my grief before I had a chance to taste them.

Claude was at work and Will was at school. The house
looked and smelled like a museum. These days, I had no
energy for anything. I felt tired, endlessly tired, and barely
able to think. Sometimes my thoughts, like a pack of
dogs, chased each other in circles for hours. Other times,
it seemed that a whole day passed without my having
thought a single thing. The four of us were still eating and
sleeping in the same room upstairs, like inmates who refuse

to leave their cells once they are freed. Life felt more manageable and closer to Hannah where her scent still lived in the sheets.

The first few weeks after Hannah's death, I moved through my days feeling numb but efficient. I had returned phone calls, written thank-you notes, and filled vases with bouquets of flowers that arrived each day. At first, an almost constant stream of visitors and mail poured through our front door. Gradually, as the flurry abated, I had started to clean. Beginning at the top of the house and working my way down, I wiped, washed, and vacuumed every surface in every room except Hannah's. Then I made lists of things yet to do and people yet to see. I might as well have written my plans in invisible ink.

It was as if I had been lowered into a vat of slow-drying cement; I had become immobile gradually, and now felt almost completely paralyzed by grief.

Breath

I WAS DREAMING, BUT I FELT AWAKE. EVERYTHING AROUND me was darker and deeper than night. I had no eyes to open. Hannah was with me. I could feel her weight on my lap and the softness of her hair on the top of her head where I rested my chin. She was leaning against me, or perhaps I was leaning against her. I held her quietly, breathing her in.

My eyes opened. I could barely see the outlines of furniture in the room. Had I been awake or asleep? I wasn't sure. I could feel Hannah's presence, lingering, as if she had just stepped away for a moment.

I closed my eyes, knowing she had been here, greedy for her to return.

Choice

BY THE SOUND OF ITS ENGINE, I KNEW THE CAR WAS coming fast. I stood on the curb, and, with a sense of calm detachment, rolled the image around in my mind. Before the unsuspecting speeder could slam on his brakes, I would throw myself in front of him.

Three months after Hannah's death, my life felt completely out of control; the pain of losing her was more than I could bear. I felt as if I were caught in a downward death spiral; there seemed to be no relief from grief. I had expected, having had a year to prepare for Hannah's death, that by now I would have a handle on things. I felt like a failure because, instead of feeling better, I kept feeling worse and worse.

My rational mind's desperate attempts to convince me that I had a lot of reasons to live kept getting blotted out by my pain. I felt detached from my body and everything else. Despite having two children I loved, despite my bond with Claude, life seemed empty and meaningless now that

Hannah was dead. The same impotence I had felt in trying to prepare for Hannah's death, I now felt in my grief.

A white sedan crested the hill and roared past. I turned my head and closed my eyes as a whirl of dust blew into my face. My body started to shake. Stepping back from the curb, I collapsed in a heap on the grass.

I didn't know what to do. All my life, whenever I had been faced with a problem, I had done what I could to control the situation. I had read about it, made lists, and carefully planned my response to it. I had coped by creating a sense of order in the midst of chaos, by finding something good in it. Now, it was as if Hannah's death had dismantled me; I could no longer think clearly. My attention span was so limited that I found it almost impossible to read. Since a life without Hannah felt pointless, planning for it or trying to find something good about it seemed obscene.

I couldn't understand why our family had been singled out for suffering. The sight of other children Hannah's age made my heart shrivel. I felt cheated by life and hated that they had lived while she had died. I knew that what had happened to Hannah wasn't anyone else's fault, and I felt deeply ashamed for feeling the way I did.

Curled up in the grass, I let the tears and frustration pour out of me. Then I slowly sat up, wiped my face with the sleeve of my sweater, and took a deep, shuddering breath. The cool autumn air crept into my lungs, filling my chest. I was surprised by its bite. I held my breath for a moment and then exhaled. It had been so long since I had felt myself in my body. I loved how good it felt. I momentarily forgot about my thoughts and began to concentrate on my breath. I inhaled again, this time more slowly. I paused, then exhaled through my teeth. I inhaled again, this time through my mouth, and exhaled quickly through my nose. I savored the fullness in my chest as I breathed, amazed to feel life coursing through me.

I realized then that my body was telling me I didn't really want to die. As I continued to breathe, I softened into an awareness that I didn't need to control my life, deny my feelings, or try to get better. I only had to allow myself to be who I was, where I was, in the moment. Life would do the rest.

Descent

IT WAS A COLD, WET NIGHT, BUT I WANTED DESPERATELY to escape the house. Our fourteenth wedding anniversary was a week away, but that hadn't stopped Claude and me from engaging in a bitter argument. Claude had wanted to make love; I had refused. Weeks of unspoken resentment had poured into the space between us. For years, this pattern of advance, rebuff, resentment, and frustration had been a source of pain and tension in our marriage, but what had felt before like a series of skirmishes now felt like a fight to the death.

I was resenting more and more Claude's expectations of me as his wife. I also knew that we had created them together. In the early years of our marriage, it was I who first believed that I would have to be perfect in order for our marriage to work. I had devoted myself to making Claude happy. Although I eventually resented his dependence on me, I had loved it, too; the more indispensable I felt, the more worthy of love I believed I was. Now, fourteen years into our marriage, Claude and I had both come to expect that a "good wife" meant hand-packed lunches, a clean, quiet house, home-cooked meals, well-behaved children, and sex on demand.

After a lifetime spent taking care of Claude and everyone else, a hungry bear was waking up in me; a fierce commitment to making something of myself was lumbering through the dark cave of my soul, sniffing cautiously in the direction of the light. I still felt mostly overwhelmed by sadness, so the moments when I wasn't suffocating were especially precious. I wanted to spend them carefully, to be honest about what I needed, to do only what really mattered to me.

For our marriage, my shift in priorities couldn't have come at a worse time. Both of us were clinging to the wreckage after Hannah's death, trying desperately to reassemble our lives. Everyone we knew, including Hannah's doctors, nurses, and social workers, had been impressed by the way Claude and I had managed to walk side by side through Hannah's illness. But now it seemed that the chasms that had always been between us were widening.

As convinced as I was that I needed to make something of my life, I was even more determined to make things work with Claude. I didn't think that I would be able to survive without him. I knew the statistics were against us; I had read that more than seventy percent of couples divorce within five years of their child's death. I wasn't willing for us to become one of them. Despite all our difficulties, Claude was Hannah's father, the only person in the world who could ever know the extent of my loss and share the depth of my grief. I would do anything to save our marriage; being alone in missing Hannah was more than I could bear.

Bending my head into the pelting rain, I stepped into the December night and began to wander through our neighborhood. Looking at the warm light spilling from other people's windows, I felt more and more desperate and lonely, as if the life that had abandoned Hannah was now, in a different way, abandoning me.

It made me sick the way everything was moving on faster than I could keep up, as if Hannah's death had already been forgotten. Why couldn't it be like a giant game of freeze tag, where everyone got temporarily frozen, not just me? While I resented that Claude had been able to take refuge in his work, that my friends were busy with their own families and lives, I had no wish to return to the way things used to be. Almost everything I'd once cared about seemed foolish and meaningless to me now.

I had no idea what I wanted; I only knew that I was terrified of being alone in it.

The fear I had been holding at bay took a deep breath and swallowed me up. I doubled over in the middle of the street. A low moan rolled out of me. I began to run toward Laurajane's house, two blocks in the other direction, pleading with God to let her be home. Stumbling across her front yard, I sloshed through an ankle-deep puddle, so numb that I barely noticed. A light was on in an upstairs room. I rang the bell, collapsed on her front step, and waited. Nothing. I rang it again and began pounding on the door, hammering my fists into the wood, ramming my shoulder against it.

Nothing. I sank to my knees, my body wracked with sobs.

Dragging myself home, I let myself in the front door and climbed the stairs to the nursery where Margaret was asleep. I sat in the dark, in Hannah's favorite chair. While the storm raged outside, I rocked mindlessly, my rain-soaked jeans staining the green upholstered seat.

I stared into nothing and stopped resisting my loneliness. It enveloped me in a pillow of darkness. I closed my eyes and felt myself descending into a sightless, soundless place. I inhaled its silence and then, opening my mouth, let out a silent scream. It was as if I were releasing all the intensity of my suffering into the world without making a sound. It poured out of me until there was nothing left but my presence, without form, suspended in the sense of aloneness that was alive in me.

I let myself rest in the stillness, felt it holding me, breathing me. I was alone but not lonely. I realized then that alone and lonely were two different things. Loneliness came from my belief that something was missing from my life; that I needed someone or something else in order for me to be complete.

But this aloneness I now felt was the fullest experience of myself that I had ever known; in it, I knew that I was at once incomplete *and* whole.

Dreaming a New Life

✿

I PUT THE KETTLE ON THE STOVE AND TOOK TWO MUGS from the cupboard as soon as I heard Laurajane's jeep pull into the driveway. I had become accustomed to her frequent, unannounced visits and looked forward to them. Today I was especially glad to see her. Last Sunday, she had reminded the congregation that Easter, the season of miracles, was coming. I wanted to know, if this was the season of miracles, when I was going to get mine.

Although I was beginning to have more moments where I inhaled the ripeness of melons in the market, laughed out loud at a joke, or bent down to wipe a scuff mark from the toe of my shoe, they felt fleeting and painful, as if a cardboard match from a cheap matchbook had lit up my solitude just long enough to burn my fingertips before I blew it out. These days, I had no desire to let go of my grief, convinced that if I did, I would also have to let go of Hannah.

The front door opened and closed, and then Laurajane's footsteps came two at a time up the steps into the living room.

"There you are," she said, giving me a kiss. "Where's my girl?"

"Taking a nap, and don't you dare wake her," I said.

"I won't," she answered, tiptoeing up the steps to Margaret's room.

While I waited for her to come back, I poured hot water into the mugs and dropped a tea bag into each one. When Laurajane returned, we sat down next to each other at the kitchen table. Laurajane took a sip of her tea and grinned at me.

"You're pregnant," she said. "I had a dream about it last night. I've had pregnancy dreams before. I've never been wrong."

I hesitated. She seemed so certain. I hated to disappoint her.

"It's not possible," I told her. "I just had my period about two weeks ago. There's no way."

Laurajane stopped smiling and studied me.

"Are you sure? I don't believe it," she said defiantly. "I've *never* been wrong."

"I'm sure," I told her.

It was true that, despite our problems and perhaps even because of them, Claude and I had crawled back into each other's arms and decided that we wanted to have one more baby. We had also agreed that it was now or never. We had just in the last month stopped using birth control; I would have been shocked to be pregnant so soon.

Two weeks later, I watched the white pad on the pregnancy test stick split in two by a thin line that deepened from china to robin's-egg to deep-sea blue.

Peeling the Onion of Grief

✧

I PEEKED INTO WILL'S ROOM TO SEE IF HE HAD FALLEN
asleep.

"Hi, Mom," he said, his voice muffled behind the comforter he had pulled up to his chin.

"How are you, Muffin?" I asked.

"Pretty good," he said. "Do you think you could lie
with me for a while?"

"Of course," I said.

Will rearranged his blue bunny and Hannah's blanket to
make room for me. He was now sleeping in the room that
used to be Hannah's. It had been his idea to make the
change. As I climbed in next to him, I noticed that he had
moved a small framed photo of Hannah from my dresser
and placed it on the table next to his bed.

The two of us lay quietly in the dark. I had almost fallen
asleep when I heard Will speak.

"Mom, how can we be sure Hannah was really dead?" His
voice was quivering. "I'm afraid she woke up in her coffin
and there's no way for her to get out!"

He started to cry. I was surprised by his concern, because he had spent so much time with Hannah's body after her death. But I also knew, from the books I had managed to read about children and grief, that a child's understanding of death changes over time as he matures.

"Oh, Muffin," I said, encircling him in my arms, "remember the policeman who came to our house afterward to officially declare Hannah dead? Remember how cold and hard her body was three days after? I'm positive she was dead."

"Are you sure it was three days after?" Will asked.

"Yes, Will, I'm sure," I said. "Hannah died on Wednesday, and her body was buried on Saturday."

"Oh," he said, wiping his tears with the sleeve of his pajamas.

"There's something else, too," he said.

"Remember how, when you told me Hannah was going to die, I said, 'From now on, whenever she asks, I'm going to let her sleep in my other bed'? Well, one time I was so mad at her for taking some of my superhero figures from my room, that when she asked to sleep with me, I told her no. I can't believe I was so mean."

Now we were both crying. It was ten months since Hannah's death, and grief was beginning to feel like an onion whose layers get thicker and more pungent the deeper you go. These days, I couldn't stop replaying the last months of Hannah's life in my head. I couldn't believe I had ever thought it would be okay to let her go. I felt guilty for everything, from the moments I had left her alone to go to the bathroom to the times when, frustrated and exhausted, I had lost my temper. I knew that Claude was filled with regrets, too. Weeks before, I had woken in the middle of the night to the sound of him weeping, our whole bed shaking as he sobbed.

I lifted Will's chin until his eyes were looking into mine.

"I'm glad you shared this with me," I said, kissing the tip of his nose. "I feel sad a lot these days. I miss Hannah, too, and I feel sorry about some of the things I said and did. But I also know I did the best I could, and I think you did, too."

"Yeah, Mom, I know that," Will said, sniffling and wiping his nose on the blanket.

"Hannah told me that human beings aren't supposed to be perfect."

"She did?" I said, surprised. "When did she say that?"

"Just the other day," he said. "Hannah and I talk about stuff. She helps me a lot and makes me not feel so sad. She says heaven is really cool, and she's not scared. They have baseball there, you know, and Hannah's on the green team. Guess what else, Mom."

"I couldn't," I said.

"Hannah is so excited 'cause now that she's in heaven she's going to grow her hair long, and she doesn't have to wait until she's sixteen to get pierced ears."

Dead Is Dead

SITTING IN THE MIDDLE OF THE FLOOR, I SORTED THROUGH the small pile of things that were all that was left of Hannah's life. I lifted her Easter dress to my nose, wanting to believe that her clothes still smelled like her, feeling sick that I was no longer sure. I was finally beginning to understand how gone she was.

A month and a half ago, in a haze of disbelief, I had slogged through the first anniversary of her death. Laurajane and fifty others gathered with us on the front lawn of our church to dedicate a small magnolia tree that had been planted there in Hannah's name. It felt like a beautiful but inadequate consolation.

I couldn't help thinking that since we had managed to survive a full year without her, Hannah should be allowed to come back. When she didn't, I spent three days in the deepest depression I had known since her death, emerging from it like a spider rescued from drowning whose legs have to be untangled before he can move on.

Two weeks later, faced with Hannah's fifth birthday, I'd

had enough of depression. Claude, Will, and I decided to celebrate by doing something we knew Hannah would love. We rented a convertible, a red one, since the guy at the counter told us they didn't have anything in pink. The four of us, Claude and I in the front seat, Will and Margaret in the back, spent Hannah's day driving around, feeling the wind in our hair.

Now, I wrapped the Easter dress, robe j's, and Hannah's first pair of red shoes in tissue paper and placed them in a box. Then I carefully laid her Band-Aid collection, sea shells, and preschool art projects on top. Closing the lid, resting the box on my swollen belly, I carried it upstairs and slid it under our bed.

These things, I decided, were too special for anyone else to use.

I stored the rest of her clothes in the crawl space above the hall, and moved her dress-up box, dollhouse, Barbies, and tea set into Margaret's room. When I finished, I lay in the middle of the floor and cried my heart dry.

Are You Looking at Me?

STANDING IN FRONT OF THE BATHROOM MIRROR, I STARED at my reflection. I barely recognized myself. My face looked more angular and worn than I remembered, my eyes focused on something I could not see. I looked tired, determined, wise. Whose form was this? I wondered. What life was it wanting to live?

A month before, in late November, Madelaine Grace had been born. Holding her for the first time, I felt complete as a mother, and knew she was the last baby I needed to bring into the world. Besides feeling a numbing gratitude, I had also felt deeply afraid. While Madelaine's birth had given me one more reason to live, it also meant I had much more to lose. I didn't want to be disappointed by life again.

I also knew that I had to start living my life. The hungry bear of my determination, which had sniffed cautiously at the light months ago, was now standing upright, pawing restlessly at the air. She could no longer wait for me to feel better, stronger, or less sad. In the sixteen months since

Hannah's death, Will had learned to read, Margaret had walked, Claude had raised money for cancer research, and Madelaine had swallowed her first gulp of the world. I no longer felt willing for life to continue on without me.

Looking into my own eyes, I saw a woman who, having been dismantled by suffering, had managed to piece herself back together. I felt a deep respect and compassion for her, for the emptiness she had known, for the strength she had found. I now knew that, just as Hannah had been able to see beyond her body's deterioration, I was much more than a bereaved mother. My anger at the world had diffused into a determination to do something purposeful and real in my life.

The grief that once threatened to swallow me up had found a home in my bones. My suffering wasn't something I was going to have to let go of; it had become part of what I had to offer, part of who I am.

Social Grace

I SAT SILENTLY BETWEEN KIM AND KATE AT A LINEN-covered table at the Newcomers' Ladies' Luncheon. They had talked me into coming this afternoon, having assured me that it would do me good. Since Hannah's death, I had resisted putting myself in social situations with people I didn't know. I still felt like a loose cannon, as if Hannah's death had left me without a polite bone in my body. I was never sure of how I would respond to the awkward and painful questions that strangers inevitably asked.

"How many children do you have?" was the most difficult. If I said "three," I felt awful for having excluded Hannah. If I said "four," the next question always was, "How old are they?"

Once people were confronted with the story of Hannah's death, almost anything could happen. It was in some of those moments that I had frequently wanted to bite someone's head off. The question that incensed me most—usually asked by other mothers—was some version of, "Did you feed her hot dogs?" I resented the implication that, since I had, I had contributed to Hannah's cancer; I also recognized the deep fear that lurked beneath the surface of their concern.

I, too, had once believed that I could protect my children from harm, control the things that happened to me and them. As a mother of three other children, part of me still wanted to believe I could. I had spent hours backtracking through every detail of Hannah's life, trying to figure out why she had gotten sick. I still longed to know if there was something else I could have, should have, done. I hadn't yet accepted that I might never know, and didn't appreciate having the question stirred up in me again and again.

Now, although I couldn't help feeling as if my real self was hiding behind a made-up, dressed-up cardboard cutout, I was beginning to think Kim and Kate might have been right to bring me here. The three of us had successfully navigated the cocktail hour, Kim and Kate sticking nervously close to my side, steering conversations toward benign subjects like the difficulty of finding a reliable gardener. I imagined they had decided beforehand that superficiality was a safer bet than subjects that could bring up words like "cancer" or "death."

Now, although the three of us had been seated at a table with seven other women, none of whom we knew, it seemed that we might get through lunch unscathed, too. Once everyone had ordered their food, a lively conversation sprang up about the hassle of getting a new driver's license when one moves to a new state.

One woman told an elaborate story of having made three different visits to the department of motor vehicles in an effort to get a decent photograph. I quietly sipped my wine and studied the faces at our table. How many of them believed, as I once had, that only "other" people's children die? I couldn't see a trace of suffering on any of them. I wondered if they would say the same about me. Despite the carefully manicured fingernails and heads of perfectly coiffed hair, I knew I couldn't know perfection by the way things looked. I knew I couldn't know suffering that way, either.

One of the women, with teased, blond hair, the one who had recently moved to New Jersey from Atlanta, broke into the conversation. Pulling a Gucci wallet from her bag, she flipped through a stack of credit cards before finding what she was looking for.

"Take a look at this," she said loudly. She handed her driver's license to the woman next to her. "I almost died when I saw it. I look like a *chemotherapy patient,* for God's sake."

Kim and Kate froze. I looked at the woman. I wanted to tell her that the most beautiful face I knew had belonged to a chemotherapy patient, but I said nothing.

I knew there had been a time in my life when I had been oblivious to suffering—my own and everyone else's. I had believed that people brought suffering onto themselves. I had felt superior to them and thought that compassion was about feeling sorry for the fact that their lives weren't perfect like mine. I now knew that I, too, had always suffered; I simply hadn't been willing or able to acknowledge it.

This big-haired woman with the chemotherapy driver's license was not my enemy. She was myself.

Belonging

SOME OF THE PARENTS WERE ALREADY STANDING. SHAKING with anticipation, I squeezed Claude's hand. I had been looking forward to this evening for a long time.

"Hannah Catherine Martell," the woman announced into the microphone. The sound of Hannah's name bounced off the beamed ceiling of the church. Claude and I stood proudly, tears streaming down our cheeks, while another candle was lit on the altar. Every pair of eyes, even those in front, had turned to acknowledge us. These people didn't have to know us personally to know where we had been; it was their story, too.

This was a different kind of graduation ceremony, a memorial service for bereaved parents hosted by a group called the Compassionate Friends. Claude and I had begun to attend their weekly meetings and, for the first time since Hannah's death, found a place where we weren't strange or special for having lost a child, where people weren't afraid of our tears or anxious for us to "move on." The weekly gatherings were also a way for Claude and me to give time to each other while keeping Hannah's memory alive. Sitting in the car afterward, no kids in sight, talking about our feelings, it was almost as if we were dating again.

In the past year, I had also begun to connect with other bereaved mothers whose children had died of cancer. One of the social workers at the hospital clinic where Hannah had been treated suggested that my experience might be able to help others. I had agreed to try. Now, fifteen of us gathered regularly in each other's home. It was the only play group I knew of where the kids played while the mothers cried.

I no longer felt special or singled out for having lost a child. Where I had once believed that suffering was something that only happened to other people, I now knew that it was a part of me that had been there all along. I had learned to have compassion for myself, and now, recognizing suffering in others, I could have the same compassion for them.

As the roll call of names came to an end, a sanctuary full of family and friends began to clap, filling the space with a swell of love and respect for the parents who continued to stand. I couldn't remember ever having felt more deeply honored. As everyone filed out and gathered for coffee in the adjoining meeting room, a few of us stood in a circle, talking about our kids.

I was in the middle of a story about Hannah when one of the other mothers broke in.

"Oh, my God," she said. *"You're the mother of the little girl with the red shoes!"*

Her name was Barbara, she told us, and her daughter Erin was two years old when she died. She had been treated in the same hospital as Hannah, in the pediatric intensive care unit where Hannah had recovered from her surgeries.

"The residents and nurses there were so great," Barbara said. "They treated Erin like she was a person in her own right. They always introduced themselves when they came into the room. And they paid attention to details that might seem silly to some people, but meant a lot to Erin—like letting her choose her own Band-Aids."

Claude and I smiled at each other and squeezed each other's hands.

Barbara continued. "The nurses told me that Erin reminded them of another little girl. They still thought about her all the time, they said, because she had changed the way they did a lot of things. They couldn't tell me her name for privacy reasons, but they always referred to her as 'the little girl with the red shoes.' "

Claude and I began to cry again, not from a place of sadness, but from a profound sense of pride and relief. It seemed that Hannah's life was making a difference in the world, in the hearts and lives of people she loved, and in many others she never knew.

COMPASSION DOES NOT FEEL sorry in the face of suffering; it knows that all suffering is its own. When we recognize this connection between us and everyone else, we know that we belong to each other; we do not suffer alone.

Wonder

*from needing to know
to letting go*

Start walking . . .
your legs will get heavy and tired . . .
Then comes the moment,
of feeling the wings you've grown,
lifting . . .

—Rumi

Thirst

❧

"DO YOU EVER WONDER, 'WHAT'S THE POINT?'" LAURAJANE asked.

She was standing with her back to our living room window, the afternoon sun pouring in behind her. She could have been mistaken for a red-haloed angel except she looked too exasperated to be holy. The thing I had come to love about Laurajane more than anything else was the way she dived right in.

"I mean, really," she continued, "what is God *thinking*? There *must* be a point. I can't believe He'd go to all this trouble for nothing."

I couldn't have agreed more. These days, feeling stronger and more determined than ever to make something of myself and my life, I was ready to tackle the two questions that had wrapped themselves around my heart and refused to let go: Why had Hannah died? Where was she now? I felt impatient, as if I knew both too much and too little at once. While I was sure that Hannah had died for a reason, I didn't know what it was. I also sensed that she was somewhere; I just didn't know where. It seemed that, no matter what I did, this was always where I ended up. I felt certain that if I could answer these two questions, everything else in my life would finally fall into place.

"I'm tired of wondering about the same things over and over again," I said. "Why don't we do something to try to figure it out?"

A week later, Laurajane and I met at my house with a few other women for the first gathering of what we eventually began to call our "Friday Morning Spiritual Group." Together, we began a search for answers. Laurajane, who had for years been exploring other religious traditions as a way to deepen her understanding, served as our informal leader. At her suggestion, we started reading and discussing books on topics ranging from dream interpretation to psychic phenomena to the inherent wisdom in other religions. Where I once had met with friends to drink coffee and gossip, I was now drinking coffee and talking about reincarnation.

I felt as if I were a tiny bird, pecking from the inside of my shell, just about to hatch. I felt drastically different on the inside, while the exterior of my life still looked much the same as it had before Hannah got sick. After all I had been through, I felt frustrated that I had almost nothing to show for it. I longed for my outer life to be more passionate and spontaneous, to reflect the growing sense of freedom and boldness I was feeling inside. But I was also hesitant to make too many changes too soon. A sense of stability had only recently returned to my life; there was something that felt comfortable and safe about the way things had always been.

Although I was hesitant to step fully into a new life, the books I was reading and the conversations I was having were opening something in me. I was learning a language for experiences I had lived through that had seemed, until now, beyond words. The part of me that had always felt like an outsider, different from most people I knew, felt less strange to me now. While I still felt a deep relationship to my Christian faith, I now felt free to experiment with other ways to express and experience my devotion. I began to keep a journal of my dreams, light candles, and burn incense, things I had done instinctively as a teenager but had abandoned years ago, as if I had to "grow up."

When I shared my enthusiasm with Claude, he wasn't impressed.

"You and those friends of yours are just a bunch of crazy weirdos," he said. He was only half-joking.

Although a part of me believed he might be right, I wasn't about to give up the search. Like a parched desert pilgrim who had caught the scent of a leafy oasis in the distance, there was no stopping me now.

Fragility

THE CHRISTMAS PARTY AT CLAUDE'S OFFICE WAS FINALLY winding down. Everyone had enjoyed cookies, punch, and square dancing in the cafeteria, and waited in a long line to visit with Mrs. Claus and Santa. It was late; many families had already gone home. The hall was empty as we walked to the elevator. I was carrying Maddy, while Will chased Margaret in circles around Claude and me.

From the other end of the hall, a woman and a young girl began walking toward us. As they got closer, Claude recognized the woman as one of his coworkers. We stopped to introduce ourselves and then all of us, including the woman and her daughter, stepped into the elevator. As the doors slid shut, the woman glanced around.

"Aren't you missing one?" she asked.

Claude looked at Will, Margaret, and Madelaine, and then at me.

"No," he said, turning to the woman. "What do you mean?"

"That's curious," the woman said, her brows knitted,

"I'm *sure* when I first saw you in the hallway, you had four children with you, not three."

Claude and I looked at each other, both wondering the same thing. I wanted more than anything to believe this was a visitation from Hannah, but I was afraid to look at it too closely. Even a breath of doubt might disturb such a fragile connection.

Dreamweaver

I PULLED INTO THE DRIVEWAY AND PARKED. LEAVING THE girls buckled into their car seats so they couldn't wander off, I began to unload the flats of impatiens and pansies from the back of the car. It was spring. The same button-wood trees that had unfurled their nubs of green while Hannah was alive were doing it again. Now it was Margaret and Madelaine, instead of Hannah, who loved to visit the pond, feed the ducks, and wave to the giant magnolia tree. I felt as if I were ascending a spiral staircase where the view kept returning, but each time my own perspective had changed.

As I finished unloading the flowers, I brushed the soil off my hands and then noticed that someone had hung a large plastic bag around the handle of our front door. Probably some hand-me-down clothes for the girls, I thought. I picked the bag up and peeked inside. I was wrong. Inside was a note and what looked like a rolled-up piece of wool. I read the note first.

Dear Mrs. Martell,

This rug is for you. It is from your daughter Hannah. Please do not think I am strange. Nothing like this has ever happened to me. Although you and I have never met, I heard about Hannah when one of my daughters attended Meadow Flower preschool. A few years ago, I learned the art of rug weaving, and decided to make a rug for each of my four girls. When I first started this rug, I had believed it was for one of them. It wasn't long before I realized I was wrong. Every moment I spent with it, I found myself thinking about Hannah. In some way I cannot explain, I knew Hannah wanted me to weave this rug for you as a message from her. In the past year, as the two of us worked on this rug together, Hannah has changed the way I feel about life after death. I am no longer afraid. I feel blessed. Hannah loves you very much. Thank you for being her mother.

Love,
Joann

As I unrolled the rug, I felt my wondering mind unravel. The background of the rug was the exact, unusual shade of teal as the carpet in our house. There, in the middle of it, a barefoot, blond-haired angel hung suspended in a starry sky. In her hands she clasped a large, pink rose—Rose, the name Hannah had chosen for Margaret's middle name.

Standing in the driveway, I began to cry. This, I knew in my heart, *was* a message from Hannah, and I loved that she had dropped it into the middle of a "nothing special" day.

Exhale

MARGARET HAD TURNED THREE OVER THE SUMMER. SHE and Madelaine, like two rhesus monkeys, were always together; everywhere Margaret went, Madelaine went, too. These days they were asking a lot of questions about their big sister, Hannah. It was time, I decided, to show them the box of Hannah's special things. I had just pulled it out from under the bed when the phone rang.

"Wait a second, girls. I'll be right back," I said.

"Okay, Mommy," they replied.

I should have known better. I raced downstairs and picked up the phone. It was the mother of one of the boys from Will's basketball team, calling with directions to this evening's game. I wrote the directions down, and then asked her about the end-of-season pizza party we were planning for the team. As the two of us talked, I lost track of time. Suddenly I remembered that Margaret and Madelaine were waiting for me. I had just said good-bye when I heard the girls coming down the stairs.

"Don't I look beautiful, Mommy?" Maddy said.

"And me too, Mommy," Margaret chimed in.

I hung up the phone and turned.

Maddy was wearing Hannah's pink-flowered robe j's. The nightgown was so long on her that she had to hike it up around her waist to keep from tripping. She stuck one foot out toward me.

"Look, Mommy, they fit just perfect," she said. Sure enough, Hannah's red shoes were on her feet.

"I helped Maddy buckle them," Margaret said proudly.

I turned to Margaret. I had been so distracted by Maddy's getup that I hadn't noticed hers. Every inch of exposed skin, from her head to her toes, was covered with Hannah's Band-Aid collection. The two of them stood there, grinning at me.

I hadn't realized until now that I had been holding my breath since Hannah died; afraid that my memories of her would vanish if I wasn't able to preserve the magic in these special things. Now that the spell had been broken, I knew there was a lot more life in those Band-Aids, robe j's, and red shoes yet to be lived. I had to let Hannah's memories out of the box, and I had to let myself out, too. Looking at Margaret and Madelaine beaming at me, I didn't know whether to laugh out loud or burst into tears.

"You two look gorgeous," I said finally, kneeling and opening my arms. As the two of them fell giggling into my lap, I added, "And Hannah would think so, too."

Given

I COULDN'T TAKE MY EYES OFF IT. STANDING IN FRONT OF Monet's masterpiece in New York City's Metropolitan Museum of Art, I realized that his bold whips of paint had captured the moment when a vase of sunflowers on a crimson cloth is all you need from God.

The next day I bought a small set of acrylic paints, a few brushes, a stretched canvas, and a how-to book. I spread sheets of newspaper over the dining room table, filled a small bowl with water, dabbed small buttons of paint on a paper plate, and began to mix the colors. I took my time, letting each step lead me.

I started sketching, light gray pencil on white canvas, and watched a sturdy wood cabin settle into a valley of rolling hills, surrounded by a mountain of trees. Gradually a stream emerged, its white water spilling over rocks in the bend, then slowing to deep, cool eddies where it swung past the house. I built a tiny well, complete with an oak dipping bucket, and added a well-worn flower-edged path that led to the cabin's back door.

I touched the first stroke of paint to the canvas tentatively, then got bolder with each subsequent one. The colors on the tip of the brush swallowed the pencil drawing, leaving me to trust, not my plan, but the vision that had inspired it. The more patience I had with the process, the more it had to teach. I learned that a leaf is a mosaic of light and green, that a roof of cedar shakes offers hairline cracks of gold to the afternoon sun. Even mistakes were transformed on the canvas: When too much blue was accidentally mixed into the yellow, mossy shadows I hadn't known were there emerged around the rocks in the stream.

As I painted, I felt completely alive, filled with a sense of joy that was not oriented to time or place. I remembered watching Hannah as she set the table for the tea party, and knew that I had finally accepted her invitation to participate fully in my life. It was the quality of presence and attention that I brought to what I was doing, not the activity itself, that made it what it was.

Two months later, I signed my name in the bottom right corner and leaned the canvas against the window above the kitchen sink. I watched Claude through the window, pushing Margaret and Madelaine on the swings. As the girls squealed with delight, soaring in and out of a warm patch of sun, I remembered my fingerpainting afternoon with Hannah. I could almost see the drips of red, blue, yellow, and green winking at me from the grass.

Gratitude

I WAS A BLOCK AWAY FROM THE TRAFFIC LIGHT, AND IT WAS red. I was late and didn't want to slow down. Just before I lifted my foot off the accelerator, the light turned green.

"Thank you," I breathed.

These days, tired of trying to figure it all out, I had stopped praying "please, please, please" and had started saying "thank you, thank you, thank you" instead. Beginning with the obvious blessings in my life—my kids, my friends, my health, the effort Claude and I were putting into our marriage—once I started, I found that I couldn't stop. The more I looked, the more I found. Soon I was thanking everything: trees for their shade, sweaters for their comfort, dogs for their fur.

Gratitude had begun to transform the way I saw and experienced my life. Because of it, I could see that each moment contained something to be thankful for, even if it was simply the gift of another breath. I was reminded of Hannah and the way she had harvested kernels of joy almost everywhere she looked. This practice of being present with what was happening was far more than an exercise in positive thinking; it was a return to the deep stillness she had shared with me.

Within that stillness, I began to realize an even more awesome thing. No single moment stood on its own; each was a combination of all those that came before and all those that would come after. There was a pattern, an intelligence, in the way they were woven together that seemed to suggest that I was not living my life; my life was living me.

Sea Change

I WALKED ALONG THE EDGE OF THE WATER, SAVORING THE sliding crunch under my feet. I loved the ocean, and I felt humbled by its expanse and relentlessness.

I was filled with a sense, both frightening and exhilarating, that everything in my life needed to change. In the years since Hannah's death, I had wriggled out of the claustrophobic expectations I had once had for myself. Now I longed to have a clearer sense of purpose, to live a life that included more of me.

Although Claude and I were still trying to save our marriage, our love, as real and unstable as shifting sand, was eroding beneath our feet. Both of us were desperately unhappy with the way things were but couldn't agree on what we needed to do to change them. I still couldn't imagine myself without Claude; divorce seemed like a faraway option. While I felt desperate to let go of the things in my life that were no longer working, I was terrified of losing everything that still mattered to me.

Sitting down on the edge of a dune, I leaned back into its curve. I closed my eyes and listened to the pounding of my heart over the crash of the waves on the beach. I inhaled the stiff wind and licked my lips, tasting the salt on my tongue. I lay quietly, letting the immensity envelop me. I felt small, infinitely small, and yet fully embraced, held. I could feel the tide of my life sucking me away from my old ideas about who I was supposed to be. I longed to surrender to it, but first I needed to be certain that wherever it was going to take me, Hannah would be there, too.

I heard the squawk of a gull just above me. I opened my eyes and sat up.

Shading my eyes with my hand, I squinted into the brightness of the afternoon sun. The brown mottled form with its expanse of white wing swooped and dived toward me. As he dipped and juked, the bird's brown beaded eyes never left mine. He landed on the sand a few feet in front of me. The two of us quietly studied each other. At first glance, he looked like a thousand other seagulls, but as I continued to stare at him, I noticed that his belly was whiter than most, only the tips of his wing feathers were dipped in brown, and his right leg was slightly mangled. He winked one eye and then ruffled his feathers. I realized, as I looked at him, that he was as common and singular as me.

I knew then that the same mystery that hung the moon, turned the earth, and replenished the sea had given life to Hannah, made this seagull and me; it was the source of everything, arising and falling away, constantly changing and forever unchanged. Whatever I did, wherever Hannah was, the two of us were forever part of each other. It wasn't just a poetic fantasy, designed to comfort me; it was the truth.

I could give up trying to figure everything out. There was no single, right answer to the questions I was asking; their uncertainty, fullness, and mystery simply had to be lived.

Harvest

MARGARET AND MADELAINE WERE STRAPPED INTO THEIR CAR seats in the back. Will was in the front next to me. I lifted my foot from the accelerator as the car ahead slowed to make a left turn.

"Mommy, *look!*" Maddy cried excitedly, pointing her finger and wiggling in her seat. "That's where Hannah and I played in heaven before I was born!"

She was pointing to Hannah's favorite house, the light pink one with dark pink trim.

I had no idea how she knew, and didn't need to, either. I received it simply as a gift from Hannah's life, evidence of the unfathomable mystery that lives in all things.

Looking back, I realized that through the last year of Hannah's life and in the three and a half years since her death, my faith had been patiently ripening. It was in this single, exquisite moment that it finally released its hold on the uppermost branch and dropped, plump and juicy, into my lap.

Dance

THE PINK-FROSTED CAKE WITH ITS CLUSTER OF WHITE candles sat in the middle of the breakfast table. Today was Hannah's eighth birthday, and we would be celebrating just as we had every year since the day of the red convertible. Before they left for work and school, Claude and Will had blown up three bags of balloons, which were now hanging in bright bunches alongside the tissue paper streamers that swooped from each corner of the room. Margaret and Madelaine had been happy to "help" by unwinding miles of cellophane tape from the dispenser, but when I stopped to load the breakfast dishes into the dishwasher, they began to jump up and down, begging me to hurry. Hannah's birthday wasn't the only special thing about today; it was also Margaret's and Madelaine's first day of ballet.

I had known what this day would look like ever since I dreamed of being the mother of a little girl. My daughter, like the others in her class, would wear a light pink leotard and light pink tights. She would carry her light pink ballet slippers to class in a black patent leather case. Her hair would be swept into a neat ponytail, fastened with a pink satin bow. In my dream, the other moms and I smile proudly, and they all look pretty much like me. We wear tailored slacks, crisp cotton shirts, leather flats, gold watches, bracelets, and earrings. Our hair is pulled back into sleek barrettes; our younger children, the babies in their strollers, are clean, burped, and sleeping.

Yes, I knew the way the first day of ballet was supposed to look, and this *definitely* wasn't it. Madelaine's leotard was light pink, but it was covered with chocolate and last night's spaghetti dinner; she had worn it nonstop for two days, too excited even to take it off before bed. Her pink tights and slippers would match the other little girls', but her hair was already escaping from a garish pom-pom, fluorescent green, pink, and blue. Instead of a black patent leather bag, she carried her shoes and Margaret's in a yellow vinyl tote filled with the books and Barbie dolls she had packed "just in case."

As for Margaret, she had pooh-poohed my suggestion of a pink leotard and chosen to wear a dance costume from her dress-up box instead. Its electric-blue sequins and shimmering, multicolored tutu clashed only slightly with the red tights underneath. She wore sparkly silver bedroom slippers that looked like ballet slippers but weren't, and a rhinestone tiara fit for Cinderella.

Catching our reflection in the hall mirror, I hesitated. No matter what the other mothers would be wearing today, I knew that my long skirt, black leather boots, and red wool wrap would look as out of place as Margaret's sequins. Where had that other woman—the one I was in my first-day-of-ballet-class dream—gone?

Suddenly a voice in me made itself heard: "Maybe you should change your clothes into something more appropriate. Or at least insist that Margaret and Madelaine change theirs." I almost laughed out loud. This, I knew, was the voice of that other woman, the one who had always been concerned about what other people might think. *She* was afraid, but *I* wasn't.

As I stood in front of the mirror, gazing at the picture we made, I felt the sides of the box I had been living in for years drop off and fall away. I knew then that part of me would always be afraid of getting hurt, making mistakes, or not being loved. I didn't have to wait for my fear to go away. Like my suffering, it was simply part of who I am.

I turned to Margaret and Madelaine. "You two look gorgeous," I said.

"You do, too, Mommy," they said, giggling.

"Then what are we waiting for?" I said. "Let's go!"

Hannah had taught me that there is a death more painful than the one that took her body from this world: a soul suffocated by fear leaves too many joys unlived. As I watched Margaret and Madelaine march into dance class, smiling, their heads held high, I knew the magic of Hannah's red shoes had finally come full circle. She had not only given this gift to me; she had given it to her sisters, as well.

Remembering

I WAS ASLEEP, SUSPENDED IN A SILENCE WHERE NOTHING was present or happening. Something broke through the surface. The stillness let go. I floated upward, toward consciousness. I wasn't alone. I drifted slowly, gently, toward this other. My eyes were closed. I was not afraid. I heard her breath and felt the patience in her waiting, and knew she was standing beside me, next to the bed. My eyes were still closed. I let them be closed. She waited. I opened them.

She stood in the first light, smiling quietly, as if she had known all along, and still knew. It was spring, she was sick, and we had already been told she was dying.

"Mommy," she said, "I had a dream."

I lifted the covers and felt the warmth of a good night's sleep escaping. She climbed in, wiggled her body close to mine, and turned to face me.

"Mommy, I had a dream," she repeated, "a very very *special* dream."

Our faces were almost touching. She paused, her eyes shining, as if she was about to spill a secret.

"I dreamed that God and His angels came and picked me up and carried me into His world!"

She clapped her hands.

"Mommy," she exclaimed excitedly, "wouldn't that be so great?"

She threw her arms around my neck. I held her as close as I dared.

Epilogue

SEVEN YEARS AFTER HANNAH'S DEATH, MANY THINGS HAVE changed.

Claude and I did divorce. For me, our parting was both painful and inevitable. After weeks of soul-searching and truth-telling, the two of us sat at our kitchen table and drafted our own custody and settlement agreement. Just as we had done many times before, we used Dr. Markoff's rule and made the best decisions we could with the information we had at the time.

For the rest, I have walked into the life I sensed was there all along; its foundation is the stillness that emerged in my last year with Hannah, which has continued to deepen in me. My life today, which includes a new marriage, is ripe with the exhilaration of living with the unanswered questions.

Will, Margaret, and Madelaine are flourishing; in part, I believe, because of Hannah's continued presence in their lives. Will still talks to Hannah most nights before falling to sleep. Margaret and Madelaine speak proudly and often of their "big sister."

Hannah's magnolia tree, planted in front of our church, bloomed the first year. It has become a place of remembering and return for those who loved Hannah. Angel and butterfly ornaments and a child's plastic bead necklace still hang on its lower branches; bouquets of flowers are delivered to it on her birthday and on the anniversary of her death.

Hannah's red shoes were never returned to the box under my bed. They continued to click and dance through life on Madelaine's feet until the patent leather on the toes was rubbed off, the straps split at the buckles, and the heels were almost gone. The image of them continues to live in my heart, a timeless reminder of Hannah's bright spirit.

Acknowledgments

I AM COMPLETELY UNAPOLOGETIC IN MY GRATITUDE TO everyone who has been a part of this book, its wisdom, and its story. To those I have named here and to the many more I haven't, I open my arms and heart to you, and bow.

To Toni Burbank, my editor at Bantam, my deepest respect and gratitude to you for your clarity, generosity, and integrity. Your fierce commitment to this book and to me is a manifestation of grace in my life, and I know it. Thanks, too, to Beth Rashbaum, Barb Burg, Susan Corcoran, and many more at Bantam for the enthusiastic support and attention you continue to give this project.

To B.G. Dilworth, my agent, it is an honor and a joy to be working with you. Thank you for your unwavering faith in this book and everything it represents. Your open heart, sharp intellect, and willingness to dream outside the box continue to inspire my work and my vision of what is possible in it. To Debra Evans, this book's doula, I celebrate both your intuition and your willingness to act on it.

To Mark Matousek, China Galland, Jeremiah Abrams,

and Joan Oliver, thank you for your invaluable editorial input. The love and delight I experience as your friend is irrepressible and irreplaceable. To Jane Hirshfield, thank you not only for your thoughtful beauty and friendship, but for opening me to the poetry that lives in my heart. To Father Dunstan Morrissey, thank you for allowing my work to ripen in the solitude and sanctity of Sky Farm. To Dr. Clark, my high school English teacher, this book is what it is because you refused to give me A's until I did my best. Thank you for that.

To Jennifer Welwood, your friendship is a source of light in my life. To John Welwood, I am deeply nourished by the integrity and heart you pour into your continued search for what really matters. To Palden, I bow to you and the silence where we meet. To Rahim, thank you for so gracefully receiving, as you put it, "the silken whack of my angelic Zen stick." To Susan Shannon, it is a joy to walk along the path of devotion with you. To Florence Falk, thank you for your friendship and wisdom. To Diane Berke and Tony Zito, your friendship and generous hospitality allow my visits to New York City to be both more frequent and more fun.

To Mary and Phil Lore, I will always be grateful for the way the two of you walked through the fire with me. To John, Kaitlin, and Samantha, thank you for sharing your home and your hearts.

To Amy Fox, Vanda Marlow, Kath Delaney, Gary Malkin, Nick Hart-Williams, and Jeff Hutner, your friendship and support of me and my work goes far beyond the call of duty. To Wendy Perry, thank you for opening your home to Roger and me, my children, and my work. To Farhad and Mina Nawab and John Salz, I thoroughly enjoy the simplicity of our café friendship and the thought-provoking conversations we share. To Darlene at Donut Alley, much gratitude for the glazed and jellied inspiration you contributed to the long hours I sat in front of my computer.

To Dr. Peri Kamalaker, Dr. Joel Edman, Dr. Mark Markoff, Dr. Joel Brockstein, Dr. Bekele, Dr. Saad, Dr. Bagtas, Jill Kurnos-Wichtel, Susan, Nurses Pat, Katie, Amy, Bridget, Kathy, and others whose names I cannot recall but whose faces I cannot forget, I will be forever grateful for the degree of care and compassion you offered Hannah and our family. To the Christ Church United Methodist congregation in Fair Haven who prayed for us, cooked for us, and supported our family through Hannah's illness and after her death, particularly Martha and Rich Wagner, Dave, Maureen, Allison and Sara Squires, Nancy Farr, Bonnie Hallowell, Karen Ganson, and Pat Magowan, thank you.

To Laurajane Baker, your friendship and love continue to live in me. To Ralph and Carolyn Baker, thank you for allowing me to include Laurajane's life and laughter in this book. To the Fair Haven community, particularly Rhea and Fred Harris, Bob and Loukia LoPresti, Daryl and Tom Ley, Brenda Jacobson, Meaghan Ladd, Jamie Sussel-Turner, Nancy Sheridan, Maureen Campion, Nina Fisher,

Joan Forsythe, Rhett Castner, and the Meadow Flower Nursery School, thank you. To Kim Montella, Kate Shevitz, Lili Carroll, Ann and Mark Orr, Barbara and Jimmy Shaw, you were there, and I will always be grateful for that.

To all the children whose lives live on in the hearts of those they loved, including Scott Lore, Danielle Markoff, Erin Barbolini, Kimberly Pertrillo, Ryan Saberon, Bryce Ziegler, David Binaco, Stephen Verdicchio, David Vander-bilt, Sara Appelbaum, Cliff Dainty, Tushar Bhatnagar, Margaret Rose Delatore, Debbie Steup, Pamela Mullen, and Anthony Martell, I bow to you and your moms.

To Claude, I am grateful to you as Will, Hannah, Margaret, and Madelaine's dad, and respect the way that each of us continues to do the best we can with what we know. To the rest of the Martell family, including Wilbur and Helene Martell, Marien and George Kissling, Susan Martell, Ruth and Larry Allen, Charles and Cindy Martell, Julia Martell-Schnaar and Rod Schnaar, Molly and Alan Lynchosky, and Diana Martell, thank you for the unique place that each of you had in my life.

To Yann Housden, Gladys Housden, Mark and Elke Housden, and Claire and Ian Stone, thank you for opening your lives and hearts to me.

To my parents, Ron and Lenore Schlack, you have never stopped reminding me how capable and loved I am. This book is a testament to your unwavering love and support of me and each other. To the rest of my family, includ-ing Diana and Chris Root, Laura and Brock Albaugh, Ben

Schlack, Karl and Marilee Schlack, Larry and Marilyn Schlack, Betty Hoodak, and Kathleen and Lou Roehrig, thank you, thank you, thank you.

To Will, Hannah, Margaret, and Madelaine, each of you is a fount of wisdom, love, and beauty in my life. It is my greatest joy to be your mother.

To Roger Housden, my husband, my love, when you looked into me the first time we met, I knew that I had finally been seen. Thank you for every way that you so gently and fiercely supported me and this book. I know that it stands in its fullness because of you. I am grateful for everything you are, all that you have given, and for our love, as timeless and inconsequential as a last breath.

About the Author

MARIA HOUSDEN is a lecturer, author, and passionate advocate for quality of life at the end of life. From 1995 to 1999, Maria served on the Board of Directors of the Kimberly Fund, a nonprofit organization that raised money for families of children facing life-threatening illnesses. In addition, as part of her commitment to helping others learn to live life more fully, she has led groups of women on contemplative, silent journeys through Death Valley.

The mother of three children in addition to Hannah, Maria is a native of Traverse City, Michigan. She and her husband, Roger, live in a beautiful log cabin in Woodstock, New York. You can reach Maria by e-mail at hannahsgift@juno.com.